RECIPES FROM CORSICA

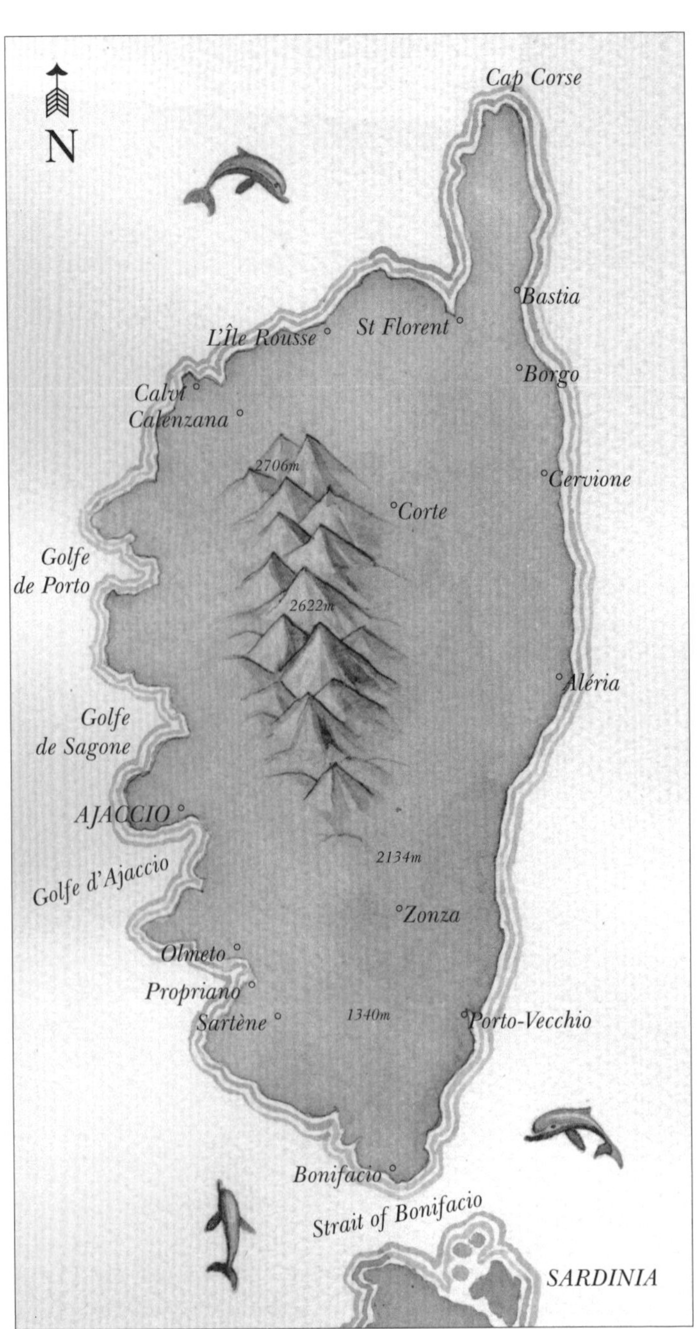

CORSICA

drawn by James Stewart

RECIPES FROM CORSICA

ROLLI LUCAROTTI

Illustrated with sketches of Corsica
by
Gilles Charbin

PROSPECT BOOKS
2004

First published in Great Britain in 2004 by Prospect Books, Allaleigh House, Blackawton, Totnes TQ9 7DL.

British Library Cataloguing in Publication Data:
A catalogue entry for this book is available from the British Library.

ISBN 1-903018-27-7

Printed in Great Britain by Kingfisher Print, Totnes, Devon.

CONTENTS

For Charlie

PREFACE

I decided to write a book of recipes of Corsican food after being unable to find one for a friend who was visiting this lovely island. I spent two years searching for and testing recipes and would like to thank my family and many friends who tasted and commented on the results. Particular thanks must go to Cathy Texier for her careful and thorough explanations of pork recipes and to Marcelle Stefanelli for many other contributions. The late Dorothy Carrington was always ready, over our weekly cup of tea, with advice and encouragement. And special thanks to my mother who instilled in me a love of good food and who taught me how to cook, to John who encouraged me to write, and to my daughter Charlie without whose good-humoured help this book would probably never have been finished.

Rolli Lucarotti,
Ajaccio, April 2004.

LIST OF RECIPES

FISH AND SHELLFISH

INTRODUCTION

I fell under the spell of Corsica when I arrived in 1970, with my husband John and our baby daughter Charlie, aboard our catamaran *Ratu Etai*. Blown into Ajaccio harbour by a mistral, the strong wind that shrieks down the Rhône valley into the Mediterranean, we came to shelter from the rough seas and stayed for over thirty years.

At first we used the port as a winter base but as Charlie reached school-going age, we spent more and more time ashore, renting a flat on the quay and eventually selling our boat. I opened a catering business while John continued writing for television. The catering business led to my opening a restaurant and thereafter I became interested in the cookery of Corsica itself.

At that time it was almost impossible to find genuine Corsican food in restaurants. Although it was eaten at home, restaurateurs assumed that tourists would just be interested in pizzas and steak and chips. It is only in the last few years that Corsican speciality restaurants have begun to be found in every small town on the island and that Corsican produce has begun to be exported. The sheer quality of the products ensures their success, and enterprising manufacturers are improving packaging and distribution all the time.

What is more, recipes are finally being written down correctly. For years the only recipes one could find were vague in the extreme, with no oven temperatures or explicit quantities given. 'Until done' was the way most ended and it was only by trial and error that one found out when that was. I realized, somewhat belatedly, that the reason that oven temperatures were never stated was because, until fifty years ago, almost all cooking in the villages was done over an open wood fire or in the communal wood-fired oven. As for quantities, one learned by watching one's mother or grandmother. As they mixed 'some' chestnut flour with 'some' milk it was evident how much 'some' was.

The following recipes are traditional. Originally the only fats used were lard or oil, preferably olive oil, but nowadays this is often replaced with margarine or butter.

A POTTED ISLAND HISTORY

The 'Île de Beauté' (beautiful island) to the French and 'Kalliste' (beautiful) to the Greeks, Corsica is also referred to as a mountain in the sea. Sitting amid translucent, unpolluted waters, it is situated 125 kilometres south of the Gulf of Genoa, 82 kilometres west of the Italian coast (with Elba in between), a stone's throw, just 12 kilometres, from Sardinia and some 450 kilometres east of Spain. Its strategic position in the Mediterranean means that it has been constantly invaded, fought over and occupied by different peoples.

Ancient invaders included the Greeks, who founded the town of Alalia (now called Aleria) on the east coast in 540 BC, and introduced vines, olive trees and cereals to the island, the Etruscans, then Greeks again before the Carthaginians. In 260 BC the Romans arrived and eventually, a century later, conquered the whole island. They stayed until the fall of the Empire when, in the fifth and sixth centuries AD, the Vandals, Ostrogoths and Byzantines moved in, to be succeeded by the Lombards. They didn't stay long and the island was put under Papal protection, which unfortunately didn't stop the Saracens from launching attacks and incursions over the next three centuries.

In 1077 the Bishop of Pisa was sent to exercise Papal authority over the island, an authority that continued for two centuries, in spite of conflicts with the Genoese and between Genoa and the Kingdom of Aragon for regional supremacy. Genoa prevailed and ruled the island until 1729 when Corsicans rebelled and sought independence. Years of fighting followed, with even the British joining in. Finally, in 1768, the year before Napoleon Bonaparte's birth, Corsica became French.

From even this extremely potted history of Corsica, it is evident that many different influences were brought to bear on the cuisine of the island. Those readers who wish to know more of the topography and historical background can immerse themselves in Corsica's rich bibliography. Modern works include volumes in the *Rough Guide* and *Lonely Planet* series. Looking a little further back, there is the matchless book by Dorothy Carrington, *Granite Island*, first published in 1971, and Edward Lear's *The Journal of a Landscape Painter in Corsica* which came out in 1870.

CLIMATE AND TOPOGRAPHY

An important aspect of agriculture is the fact that Corsica is the only island in the Mediterranean with a high rainfall; more in fact than that of the Paris region. The rain falls mainly in the mountain ranges, which have fifty peaks of over 2000 metres (of which the highest is Monte Cinto at 2706 metres), and the many torrents and rivers that run down to the sea water the lands around them.

Add to this a temperate climate with plenty of sunshine and you have ideal conditions for cultivating the soil, although the fact that a lot of the island is made up of granite rockface limits the extent of arable land.

From the permanently snow-capped top of Monte Cinto, down through forests of maritime and Laricio pines, chestnut forests, orchards and olive groves and, finishing at sea level with palm trees and cactus plants, an enormous variety of plant life can be found in Corsica. Of the more than 2,800 species of flowering plants found on the island, 300 are native.

But perhaps the most important consideration is that over one third of the land is now a nature reserve, the Parc Naturel Régional de la Corse. There's no intensive farming here with its accompanying pollution. Instead, all efforts are being made to guarantee that traditional methods are maintained and that produce has its own label of quality and authenticity.

PEOPLE AND PLACES

Corsica has a population of around 260,000, well over half of whom live in the three major coastal towns of Ajaccio, Bastia and Porto-Vecchio. Readers will see, from the names of dishes and foodstuffs that I have given at the heads of recipes, that the Corsican language is alive and well, although the mainland government made every effort to annihilate it in favour of French. It has been taught in schools only in the last twenty years. Although the island is small, the topography is complex and the human history likewise. This is reflected by the many linguistic variations from one part of the island to another. Spellings are often dissimilar, and different words, too, will be employed. The recipe for chestnut flour and milk repeated on page 186 is just one example. Although once an essential staple supporting the hard peasant life and thus, one might think, a candidate for a single name or description, it is called *brillulis* in the north and *granahjoli* in the south of the island.

Migration to the coasts and desertion of the mountain villages, particularly from the beginning of the twentieth century, intensified after the Second World War, when the American army sprayed the mosquito-infested eastern coastline with DDT, ridding the area of the malaria that had affected it for so long. As the coast became increasingly populated, so the villages emptied, save for the elderly who retired to their family homes and certain stalwarts who clung to the traditional way of life.

In the summer the villages come to life again as a large part of the population of the two main towns, Ajaccio and Bastia, escape the heat of the coast and install themselves in their ancestral homes in the mountains; Corsicans from the mainland come home for their annual summer holidays as well as for the major religious festivals of Christmas, Easter and All Saints' Day.

THE CORSICAN KITCHEN

Traditional dishes are prepared for feast days, often varying from one village to another. The recipes are not written down but passed from one generation to the next. They are usually learnt as the children help their mothers or aunts in the kitchen, although the men are often just as knowledgeable as the women in the matter of cooking.

Until the middle of the twentieth century, cookery in the villages was based on local produce. People ate what they grew and reared in their gardens and smallholdings as the seasons changed. Food was preserved for the winter by drying, salting, pickling and smoking. Half the house was given over to the storing of food: dried fruits, chestnuts, pulses and cereals in the attic; and hams, sausages, oil, cheeses, wine in barrels, honey and jams in the cellars.

Most of the cooking was done over the open fire although dishes were sometimes baked in the communal bread oven in the village. On fête days, no cooking was undertaken, everything having been made ready beforehand.

Meals were prepared according to what was in season and generally followed a weekly pattern. Although there was nothing overly elaborate, pride was taken in the quality and freshness of ingredients and the ingenuity shown in the use of the abundant herbs that grow wild all over the island.

Nothing went to waste; a glut of tomatoes in the summer would be left to ferment in wooden barrels for a few days to

drain the fruit of their acid, and the resultant purée would be salted then spread on wooden boards in the sun until it darkened in colour. After that, it would be stored in earthenware pots, the top protected by a film of olive oil, to be used during the winter months.

Bread was baked once a week in the communal oven. Stale bread was used to make a soup of bouillon, garlic and slices of bread sprinkled with grated cheese. Often, the evening meal was simply a bowl of soup followed by cheese and, sometimes, dried fruit – though the soup in question was usually a hearty vegetable mixture flavoured with a ham bone and thickened with pasta.

Until the beginning of the nineteenth century, most islanders, apart from the very rich, ate fresh meat only on special occasions. *Cabri* (milk-fed goat) was considered the finest meat and was served at Christmas time. Milk-fed lamb was also highly rated and was usually eaten at Easter.

The Corsicans have been shepherds for centuries and still follow the practice of transhumance, moving their flocks to the mountain pastures for the summer and back down to the plains and valleys to spend the winter. The animals are kept for their milk, which is used to make remarkable cheeses flavoured with the herbs on which the animals have fed.

PIGS AND WILD BOAR

The pig held (and still holds) a place of great importance in village life. Until the 1950s most families in the countryside kept two pigs (known as *porci mannarini*), one to be killed just before Christmas and the other to be kept for the following year. The pigs were slaughtered at a later age than intensively-farmed pigs, usually over fourteen months and sometimes up to thirty-six months old. This is still the case today and produces pigs with tasty marbled flesh with a large proportion of fat. Then as now, the pigs were semi-wild and free to roam the forests during the day, feeding on chestnuts and roots, and sometimes mating with wild boars.

Nothing of the pig was wasted, from the tip of its tail to its ears. Most of it was made into sausages and hams, which were cured and dried in the mountain air or smoked over the chimney in the house. Some of the pork was eaten fresh, and the blood was made into a sort of black pudding (*boudin*). The stomach was sometimes stuffed with the chopped heart and tongue of the pig mixed with wine and herbs (*ghialaticciu*) or with chopped onions, cabbage and chard mixed with the blood of the pig (*ventra*). This was eaten at Christmas and was considered a great delicacy. The small amount of pork that was eaten fresh was quite simply prepared, grilled or fried with herbs.

The fate of the pig hasn't changed much today. *Charcuterie* is still produced all over Corsica and is much appreciated by visitors, though to keep up with increasing demand, and EU requirements, production is necessarily becoming more industrialized. Two important cured meats are *panzetta* and *prizuttu*. *Panzetta*, which is used in many of the recipes which follow, is salted and air-dried breast of pork, similar to the Italian *pancetta*. It can be also lightly smoked. The extra age of the pigs at slaughter means it is especially fatty. British readers can substitute *pancetta* (if it is readily available to them) or fatty streaky bacon. *Prizuttu* is a cured ham and looks very like its cousin, the Spanish Serrano ham. It is salted, rinsed and then rubbed with pepper or *razzica* (see the recipe below on page 140) before being air-dried for between six and eighteen months. Very large hams may take up to two years to cure.

Wild boar is hunted for its meat, which holds a high place in Corsican gastronomy. Of the 30,000 or so wild boar on the island, about 12,000 are killed annually. The hunt is a tradition and the hunter an heroic figure in Corsican folklore. The hunt is also a social occasion and it is considered a privilege to be invited to join one.

The season starts in the middle of August and continues until the first Sunday of January. Meat is usually shared between hunters but when the hunt has been prolific some may find its way into the butcher's shop. It is of an excellent quality, the wild boar having lived off the abundant herbs of the *maquis* and chestnuts from the forests that cover much of the island.

The meat is cooked in stews, pâtés and roasts, in terrines, or in sausages. It is sometimes marinated before being cooked and is often served with pasta.

Other game includes hare, pheasant, guinea fowl, woodcock and blackbirds and thrushes. These last two are now protected but are undoubtedly still eaten in private homes.

TASTES OF HONEY

Honey has held an important place in the Corsican economy from before the birth of Christ. The Romans imposed a tribute of 65 tons of beeswax on Corsica, which gives an idea of the importance of the production. Honey and beeswax were traded from the natural harbours of the island. Records do not show trading in medieval times, but it reappears in the middle of the nineteenth century with exports to Italy until the end of the century when an epidemic of acariasis struck Corsican apiculture. The industry has steadily revived since the 1970s. There are now 22,000 hives on the island, two-thirds of which are in the north. Honey is divided into six distinct varieties according to altitude and season. They are perfumed with a multitude of different plants. The varieties are Printemps, Fleur du Maquis, Miellat du Maquis, Chataigneraie, Été, Automne-hiver.

In March 1998, the all-important AOC (*Appellation d'Origine Contrôlée*) was granted to Corsican honey, a distinction that apiculturists had been seeking for twelve years and one that has not yet been awarded to any other honey in the world.

CEDRATS AND OTHER FRUITS

Citrus fruits grow abundantly on the island – oranges, lemons, mandarins and cedrats. Corsica is one of the few places in the world where cedrats (or *cédrats*, in the French spelling) are still to be found. Cedrats are citrons (*Citrus medica*), resembling a 'huge, rough lemon': the first citrus fruit to reach the Mediterranean world from Asia. The Corsican variety is especially sweet. The island is also the second-largest producer in Europe, and the largest in France, of clementines, although these have only been cultivated in quantity for the last thirty years. Firm and juicy, they account for half the value of fruit grown on the island.

Cherries and plums, particularly greengages which used to be exported to England for jam-making, grow in profusion, as do peaches, pears, medlars, cherries, nectarines, apricots and apples. Fig trees are seen in most villages and prickly pears are everywhere. They are sold, ready-peeled, in plastic bags on street corners.

Plantations of kiwis, limes and pomolos have recently been introduced on the east coast, as have avocados, with varying success.

Fruit from the strawberry tree (*Arbutus*), which grows wild in the *maquis,* is made into delicious jelly. There are wild blackberries, mulberries, myrtle-berries and strawberries, while in the 1950s cultivated strawberries and raspberries were introduced. Of course, vine terraces have criss-crossed the landscape for over two thousand years. Fruit was preserved by drying, crystallizing, making into jam or jelly, or bottling with *eau de vie* to make *ratafias*.

Chestnut forests cover large areas of the island and hazelnut and walnut trees are abundant, particularly in the region of Cervione on the east coast. Olive trees are part of the *maquis* and grow wild all over the island. Olive oil mills are being restored and the soft and fruity oil, once known as the best in the Mediterranean, can be found in local shops and markets. Almond trees are enjoying a revival too, with the cultivation of several hundreds of hectares on the east coast. Corsican almonds are known for the softness of their skins which can be peeled with the fingers.

Add to such abundance wild plants and herbs, mushrooms, snails, freshwater trout and eels – it's not hard to see how Corsican bandits managed to survive on their own in the *maquis* for years on end!

BROCCIU, PRINCE OF CHEESES

Bruccio, brocciu or *brucciu* is the most famous of all Corsican cheeses and the only one to have been given an *Appellation d'Origine Contrôlée*. Made of goat or sheep's milk, it is served very fresh, usually as a dessert, on its own or with a sprinkling of sugar and a spoonful or two of *eau de vie* (the colourless, fiery liqueur made from the residue of grapes after winemaking).

Laetitia, Napoleon Bonaparte's mother, was so inordinately fond of *brocciu* that she had several Corsican sheep brought to Paris for fresh supplies; alas, the grass on which the sheep were fed in Rueil Malmaison didn't have quite the same perfume as the herbs of the *maquis*.

The cheese is made by heating whey (*petit lait*) and adding full-cream sheep or goat's milk. A little salt is added and the milk is gently stirred and reheated. The creamy solids that rise to the surface are skimmed off and carefully placed in small woven tubs of rush (increasingly, unfortunately, of plastic) to allow the cheese to drain. Produced between November and July, to be eaten within five days of production, *brocciu* is a light, creamy mass of delicately-perfumed curds. It cannot be compared to any other curd cheese.

Brocciu is employed extensively in cooking, for omelettes, pastries and for stuffing vegetables and fish dishes. Older, slightly salted *brocciu* called *passu* is put in savoury pastries and vegetable dishes. When the cheese has hardened further, it is grated over dishes or used in soups, sometimes having been soaked in water for a few hours to soften it.

For the purpose of my recipes, fresh *brocciu* can be replaced with ricotta or a mixture of ricotta and cream cheese. Cream cheese alone is too dense, and the little grains in cottage cheese are too rubbery. Feta cheese or Caerphilly can be used to replace slightly older *brocciu*. For the harder *brocciu* used for grating, try Parmesan or any other hard cheese. Sardinian *tomme* would be the closest, or you could use a *grana* from the Italian delicatessen.

Bastelicacciu, from the Ajaccio region, is a natural cheese made of raw sheep's milk eaten while it is still young and tender. It is best, like all cheeses, when produced artisanally.

Calinzana, produce of the Niolu (in the north of the island), is a soft, square-shaped sheep's cheese with a washed crust and a characteristic slightly pungent taste.

Cuscio is a pressed cheese made of sheep and/or goat's milk, made principally in the south of the island. This is the famous cheese which after a certain time becomes filled with cheese maggots, either loved or loathed.

Niolu also produces a cheese of the same name which is considered the best in Corsica. Made of goat or sheep's milk, the cheeses are tender and can be pungent and peppery or creamy and mild, depending on their age.

Venaco, in the centre of the island, produces fine cheeses which rival those of the Niolu. Also made with raw goat or sheep's milk, they have an orange-red crust and a subtle cream-coloured interior.

Another speciality, alas rarely now seen for sale, comes from the region of Porto-Vecchio around the time of sheep shearing. Ricotta is made by heating large flat stones from the river in a wood fire until they are white hot, then plunging them into a cauldron of boiled ewe's milk. As the cream starts to form, the stones are removed and rennet and a little sugar added. When cool, this slightly smoky-flavoured curd cheese is eaten as a dessert. This ricotta is not the same as the Italian cheese of the same name.

ISLAND HERBS

'I would recognize my island with my eyes closed,' Napoleon Bonaparte famously said. One has only to step off a 'plane arriving at the airport of Ajaccio and be greeted by the scent of the *maquis*, to understand what he meant. The *maquis* is the dense shrub that covers a large part of the island, which is made up of various herbs and plants that give their particular savour to the produce and cuisine of Corsica. Here is a list of some of the many herbs to be found growing wild on the island, and their culinary uses.

WILD GARLIC OR LEEK (*u porru salvaticu*): soups, omelettes, tarts.

FIELD SORREL (*l'acetula*): soups, salads, tarts.

WILD CHARD (*bettes, blettes, biettule*): soups, tarts, pasta.

BORAGE (*a burrascia*): soups, salads, drinks.

WILD CHICORY (*lattaredda* or *lattarepulu*): herb soup, salads, tarts and many more things.

DANDELION (*e rice bice*): soups, salads, tarts.

WILD SORREL (*a romacia*): soups, pastries, cakes.

WILD ASPARAGUS (*u sparacu*): soups, salads, omelettes.

CORSICAN THYME (*l'erba barona*): soups, stews, tisanes.

ORIGANO (*a pimpanella*): pizza, stews, sauces.

CRESS (*u criscione*): soups, salads, tarts (but the wild plant is dangerous to eat because of pollution from animals).

FENNEL (*u finochju*): soups, fish, cakes, drinks.

YELLOW GENTIAN (*a genziana*): alcoholic drink.

LUPINS (*u lupinu*): seeds are used like lentils, after soaking in water for several days.

MINT (*a menta*): soups, stews, omelettes, cakes.

CALAMINT (*a nepita*): soups, stews, vegetables, sauces, pasties, pastries, sauces, etc.

WATER MINT (*pedirossu*): soups, tarts, omelettes.

POULIOT MINT (*u pulghju*): this is also known in France as *l'herbe de Saint-Laurent*, used in soups, tarts, fritters.

POPPY (*a rosula*): soups, tarts.

ROSEMARY (*u rosamarinu*): stews, meat, sauces, tisanes.

SAGE (*salvia*): soups, meat, poultry, biscuits.

NETTLES (*l'urticula*): soups, salads, tarts.

VIOLETS (*viola*): sweets and desserts.

SOUPS

There is a Corsican saying, 'Eat your soup – or jump out the window,' which sounds better in Corsican, 'O mangia a minestra, o salta a fenestra,' as it has the advantage of rhyming. What it actually means is 'Put up with it or shut up'.

It also illustrates the importance of soup in the daily diet of Corsicans up until the middle of the last century. Each region and each season had its own soup made of pulses or fresh vegetables, meat or fish, often thickened with bread, rice or pasta. Served before cheese and fruit, it often constituted the evening meal.

CORSICAN COUNTRY SOUP

Minestra Serves 6 to 8

The most the most popular of Corsican soups is a hearty vegetable soup. The choice of vegetables depends on the seasons but almost always includes dried beans, onions and carrots. A ham bone or the trimmings of a smoked ham add to the flavour. Ask your butcher or at the delicatessen counter for end pieces of ham or bacon. Herbs are important too. Choose among marjoram, sage, sorrel and parsley (not all of them). If you are in a hurry you can replace the dried beans with a couple of 400g tins of red or white beans, drained and rinsed.

200 g dried beans (borlotti or white beans)
1 ham bone or 100 g diced panzetta *or streaky bacon*
500 g potatoes
250 g carrots
1 large onion
1 stick celery
1 large leek
2 cloves garlic
3 courgettes
2 or 3 shredded leaves of Swiss chard or cabbage
2 tomatoes peeled and chopped or 1 tbsp tomato purée
2 tbsp olive oil
200 g pasta (macaroni or thick noodles)
salt and freshly ground black pepper
herbs of your choice (fresh if possible)

Soak the dried beans in cold water overnight or for at least six hours. If using a ham bone cover it with cold water, bring to the boil, drain and discard the liquid. Reserve. Peel and dice the potatoes, carrots and onions. String and slice the celery. Split and wash the leek and cut into rounds. Crush the garlic and dice the courgettes. Heat 2 tbsp of oil in a large saucepan and gently cook the onions, leeks and bacon or *panzetta* until the vegetables start to wilt.

Add the other vegetables and tomato purée and stir for a few minutes. Drain the beans and add to the soup together with the ham bone if using. Cover with water (about 2 litres) and bring to the boil. Skim the top carefully and add herbs. Lower the heat and simmer, covered, for about 2 hours until the beans are meltingly soft. Add the pasta about 20 minutes before the end of cooking time. Correct the seasoning (the ham bone is salty), scatter with chopped herbs and serve very hot with crusty bread.

Offer extra olive oil with the soup.

HOLY THURSDAY CHICKPEA SOUP

Minestra di Ceci di Jovi Santi

Chickpea soup is traditionally served on the Thursday before Good Friday: one of the reasons given is that Jesus rode through a field of chickpeas just before his entry into Jerusalem.

When I first read this recipe I was sure some ingredient had been left out so I checked with all the other recipes of the soup that I could find. They were the same so I decided to try the recipe as it was and adjust it afterwards. It was so delicious that I ate two bowls-full, though I admit that the large spoonful of pistou sauce I stirred into the second bowl gave it an added kick.

The slipperiness of the pasta is a nice contrast to the floury texture of the chickpeas. Sometimes, some of the chickpeas would have been taken out of the soup to be served separately with a vinaigrette. The bicarbonate of soda is important to soften the peas and stop any airy side effects.

250 g chickpeas
2 tbsp bicarbonate of soda
2 large cloves garlic
3 tbsp good olive oil
100 g lasagna
salt and pepper

Soak the chickpeas overnight in cold water with the bicarbonate of soda. The next day, drain and rinse the chickpeas, put into 1 ½ litres cold salted water and bring to the boil. Reduce the heat, cover and simmer for 1 hour or until the peas are soft. Halfway through the cooking time chop the garlic very finely and add to the soup together with pepper and olive oil. Break the lasagne into large pieces and add to the soup. Continue cooking until the pasta is soft. Serve the soup as it is or with grated cheese.

BREAD SOUP

Panata, pan cotto

A favourite, soothing soup, often served to children.

200 g stale country bread
2 tbsp olive oil
2 cloves garlic, crushed
thin slices of young brocciu, 'passu', *or other fresh, tender cheese*

Break the bread into pieces and put into a saucepan with 1 litre of water. Bring to the boil, season well and add the oil and garlic. Cover and cook gently until the bread has completely dissolved into the water (about 30 minutes). Slip the slices of cheese into the soup a few minutes before serving.

DRIED CHESTNUT SOUP

Minestra di castagne secce Serves 4

250 g dried chestnuts
2 tbsp olive oil
100 g pasta (noodles or small macaroni)
salt

Soak the chestnuts overnight and, the next morning, pick out any bits of skin that might be still adhering to them. Put into 1 1/2 litres of boiling salted water and add the olive oil. Simmer, covered, for 50 minutes. Crush the chestnuts slightly with a fork and add the pasta and salt. Cook until the pasta is soft and serve.

There are variations on this recipe. Pasta is not always added and sometimes the olive oil is replaced with 500 ml of hot milk.

BROAD BEAN SOUP

Minestra di fave fresche Serves 4

In the springtime in markets the first broad beans appear next to tiny new potatoes, fresh peas and tender new courgettes. At first, the broad beans are eaten raw, mixed with other vegetables as a spring salad. Later, when they get a little larger, they are made into soup.

1 ½ kilos unpodded broad beans
200 g fresh peas
1 leek
1 bunch spring onions
250 g old or new potatoes
200 g spinach or Swiss chard leaves
100 g panzetta, *cubed*
1 clove garlic
10 leaves basil (shredded)
1 tbsp olive oil
salt and pepper

Pod the broad beans and the peas, wash and slice the leek, peel and slice the onions, peel and cube the potatoes (if the new potatoes are small, don't peel them, just wash and halve), and wash and slice the spinach or Swiss chard. Cook the *panzetta* for a minute or two in the oil and then add the onions, garlic and leek. Cook, stirring, for one minute and pour in 1 ½ litres of salted water. Add the potatoes and spinach or chard and bring to the boil. Reduce heat to simmer and cook, covered, for 30 minutes. Add the peas and broad beans, season with pepper and continue cooking for another 30 minutes. Sprinkle with the shredded basil before serving.

SWISS CHARD AND BROCCIU SOUP

Minestra di brocciu e biettule Serves 4

Brocciu and Swiss chard are a favourite combination in Corsican cooking. When fresh *brocciu* is out of season it is replaced with dry *brocciu* that has been soaked in cold water overnight.

1 onion
300 g potatoes
300 g Swiss chard
2 tbsp olive oil
1 bay leaf, 2 sprigs thyme
200 g fresh brocciu *or other fresh soft cheese*
salt and pepper
4 slices of toasted country style bread

Chop the onion and cut the potatoes and Swiss chard into small pieces. Cook the onions gently in the olive oil until the onion starts to wilt. Add the potatoes, chard and herbs and 1 $^1/_2$ litres of water. Season with salt, bring to the boil and lower the heat to simmer. Cook for 30 minutes and add the pepper and *brocciu* cut into thin slices. Cook for a further 10 minutes and serve poured over the toasted bread.

PUMPKIN SOUP

Minestra viculese incu a zucca Serves 4

This comes from the town of Vico in the centre of the island.

1 kilo pumpkin
1 litre milk
salt and pepper
100 g pasta (fairly small, e.g. shells or noodles)

Peel and cut the pumpkin into large chunks and cook in just enough salted water to cover, until soft. Push through a sieve or food mill and put back into a saucepan with the milk. Season well with salt and plenty of pepper and bring back to the boil. Add the pasta and cook until it is soft.

GARLIC SOUP

Minestra incu l'agliu Serves 4

This is simple to make, economical, but also good for you, supposedly purifying the blood and warding off colds, flu and Dracula (probably everybody else too).

1 head garlic
2 tbsp olive oil
1 bay leaf
1 1/2 litres water
salt and pepper
4 slices country style bread
100 g grated hard cheese (preferably Corsican)
4 eggs, poached or soft-boiled (optional)

Peel and crush the garlic. Heat the oil gently in a saucepan and cook the garlic for a minute or two. Do not let it colour. Add the bay leaf and water and season to taste. Bring to the boil and let the soup simmer for 30 minutes. Season. Toast the bread and put one slice in the bottom of each soup bowl. Remove the bay leaf and ladle the soup into the bowls. Sprinkle with grated cheese and serve hot. If you wish, put a poached or a peeled soft-boiled egg on top of the toast before pouring in the soup.

LEEK AND RED BEAN SOUP

Minestra di fasciolu e di porri Serves 4 to 6

This lovely warming soup comes from the Niolu, a spectacular mountain area in the north of Corsica, peopled by shepherds who are unusually tall, blonde and blue-eyed for Corsicans, and rumoured to be direct descendants of the Neolithic tribe called 'Corti'.

300 g dried red beans soaked in cold water for 12 hours
olive oil or lard
150 g panzetta, *cubed*
3 medium potatoes peeled and chopped
2 medium leeks cleaned and sliced
1 tbsp tomato purée
3 crushed cloves of garlic
salt and pepper
1 bay leaf, 1 sprig of thyme, 1 sprig of rosemary

Strain the beans, cover them with 1 ½ litres of fresh water, add ½ tsp of salt and cook for ½ hour. Meanwhile heat the oil or lard in another pan and start to fry the *panzetta* cubes. Add the leeks, potatoes, garlic, tomato purée and herbs and cook gently together, stirring, for 2 minutes. Combine with the beans and bring back to the boil. Skim off any froth, cover and simmer for about 1 ½ hours. Check the seasoning and serve hot.

ONION SOUP WITH EGGS

Minestra di civolle incu ova Serves 4

A restorative soup sufficiently filling for lunch on a cold day.

1 kilo onions sliced very thinly (preferably young onions)
3 tbsp olive oil
1 small hot red chilli pepper (optional)
salt and pepper
3 or 4 eggs
4 pieces of stale or toasted country-style bread
150 g grated cheese (Corsican hard cheese)

In a large saucepan heat the oil and cook the onions slowly until they begin to brown. This is a very important step, not to be rushed, and will take about 20 minutes. Add 1 $^1/_2$ litres water, salt and pepper and the whole red chilli pepper if you are using it. Bring to the boil, lower heat and simmer for 30 minutes. Remove the red pepper. Beat three eggs together and add, stirring continuously, to the soup, or poach four eggs. You can either poach the eggs in the soup or, for a safer result, poach them separately in simmering water to which you have added a tablespoon of vinegar. Swirl the water around with a whisk before sliding in each egg. Cook them one at a time. When they are set, remove them with a slotted spoon and keep them in lukewarm water. Put a slice of stale bread or toast in the bottom of each of four soup bowls and top with grated cheese. Pour the soup over and put a poached egg into each bowl.

WOOD PIGEON SOUP

Brodi di columbi Serves 4

Wood pigeons were once very plentiful in Corsica and the following soup was often served, sometimes as a restorative to invalids or pregnant women.

1 cleaned and plucked wood pigeon
1 or 2 tomatoes seeded, skinned and chopped
2 leeks, sliced
2 large carrots, chopped
1 stalk of celery, chopped
2 crushed cloves garlic
1 bay leaf, 1 sprig thyme
1 $^{1}/_{2}$ litres water
salt and pepper
150 g fine vermicelli

With the exception of the vermicelli, put all the ingredients into a saucepan and bring to a boil. Skim the soup, lower the heat and simmer for 35 to 45 minutes. Remove the wood-pidgeon (to eat apart), bring the soup back to the boil and add the vermicelli. Cook until the vermicelli is soft and serve very hot.

Boiling fowl were cooked in the same way although the cooking time would have been increased to 90 minutes.

FISH SOUP

Suppa di pesci Serves 6 to 8

This recipe for fish soup comes from a summer which I spent working as a chef in a restaurant in Campo Moro, a fishing village in the south-west of the island. The fish were straight from the sea in front of the restaurant and often, disconcertingly, some of the smaller fish were still alive. The red wine gives the soup a robust flavour. In the south of France or Corsica you will find fish for soup in any fish market. It is sold as 'Soupe' and is surprisingly inexpensive. It consists of small shellfish and various rock fish. The smaller fish are not usually gutted for the soup and the heads are left on, as the whole thing is later pushed through a food mill thus leaving shells and bones behind.

1 kilo mixed fish and shellfish (mussels, clams, queen scallops)
1 leek, cleaned and chopped
1 onion, chopped
3 cloves garlic, crushed
1 medium potato, peeled and sliced
2 tbsp tomato purée
3 glasses red wine
2 bay leaves, 2 sprigs thyme
2 tbsp olive oil
salt and black pepper
toasted croûtons rubbed with garlic

Wash the fish briefly and scrub any mud or sand off the shellfish. Heat the olive oil in a large saucepan and start cooking the onion, leek, garlic and shellfish. Cook, stirring, for a minute and add the potato, tomato and herbs. Put in the rest of the fish, red wine and 1 ½ litres of water. Add salt and black pepper and bring to the boil. Lower the heat and simmer, covered, for one hour. Put the soup through a food mill. This is tiresome but does give the best results. You can also blend the soup but you would still have to push it through a sieve. Serve piping hot with a *rouille*, slices of day-old French bread toasted in the oven or under a slow grill, and cut cloves of garlic to rub on the bread.

ROUILLE

4 large cloves garlic
2 small red chilli peppers or 2 tsp chilli purée (sold in Asian food stores, and many French supermarkets, as Sambal Oolek)
3 slices of crustless white bread soaked in water and squeezed out
olive oil
fish stock
salt

Crush the garlic with a little salt in a mortar, then add the chillis and continue pounding. Add the bread to the mixture and combine well together. Gradually add the oil as though making a mayonnaise until the mixture is quite thick. Then you can thin it out with a little of the fish broth until it is creamy.

Alternatively, if you're in a hurry, just add the crushed garlic and chilli to some mayonnaise. See the recipe below, on page 69.

FIRST COURSES AND CANAPÉS

ANCHOVIES IN OIL

Anchiuve inca l'oliu

For this recipe you will need whole salted anchovies which are sold in wooden barrels in markets in France, but you should be able to find them in tins or jars.

500 g anchovies
4 cloves garlic, finely sliced
1 bay leaf, 2 sprigs thyme, 2 sprigs rosemary
freshly ground black pepper
olive oil to cover

Wash the anchovies under running water and remove the fillets. Place these into a jar or plastic box with a lid. Intersperse with the garlic slices and herbs and cover with olive oil. Grind some pepper over the top and seal tightly. Keep in a cool place and eat after a month.

AUBERGINES IN OIL

Mirizani incu l'oliu

I like serving these delectable pieces of aubergine with drinks or as part of an antipasto, together with a red pepper salad.

1 kilo aubergines
1 glass of vinegar
1 bay leaf, 2 sprigs thyme
1 small red chilli pepper
salt and pepper
olive oil to cover

Cut the aubergines into 2 centimetre cubes. Put the vinegar into a saucepan and add enough water to cover the aubergine pieces. Bring to the boil and add the aubergines. Bring back to the boil and cook for 5 minutes. Strain and let the aubergines drain for at least four hours. Put into a sterilized jar with the herbs, seasonings and red chilli pepper and cover with the oil. Cover the top of the jar with greaseproof paper and put the lid on. Leave for a month before eating.

It's important to sterilize the jars well. To do this, boil the jars for 10 minutes, remove with two forks and turn upside down on to a clean cloth to dry.

MUSHROOMS IN OIL

Funzi incu oliu

Corsica is paradise for mushroom enthusiasts. All kinds of mushrooms are to be found including quite a few that seem to be unknown anywhere else. Mushroom hunts take place on most Sundays after a day of rain and whole families often join in. Fertile sites are kept a closely guarded secret and on Monday mornings the chemists (all of whom have taken a special course in mushroom identification), are bombarded with anxious inquiries as to the toxic nature or not of Sunday's haul.

There are several strict rules to follow. Never eat any mushrooms of which you are not absolutely sure. Never pull a mushroom out of the ground, but instead cut the stem. Don't carry mushrooms in a plastic bag and certainly don't mix unknown mushrooms with ones you intend to eat. And, if it's the hunting season, wear brightly coloured clothes and make a lot of noise so that you don't get mistaken for a wild boar.

Arlette and her husband have lived in Corsica for many years. She is a keen mushroom huntress and excellent cook and has often served us these lovely marinated mushrooms, with drinks, on her terrace overlooking the Golfe d'Ajaccio. She always uses little orange mushrooms called *lactaires délicieux* (*Lactarius deliciosus*, saffron milk cap) or *sanguines*, but concedes that one could use small ceps, also known as *bouchons*, or small cultivated button mushrooms.

1 kilo mushrooms
4 cloves garlic
small glass of vinegar
2 bay leaves, 4 sprigs thyme
salt and pepper
enough oil to half cover the mushrooms (half and half olive oil and corn oil)

Wipe the mushrooms with a damp cloth and cut them into quarters if they are large. Put them in a saucepan with the oil, peeled cloves of garlic, the herbs, salt and lots of freshly ground black pepper. Cook over a very low heat for about half an hour or until the oil is orange (if you are using *lactaires délicieux*). The mushrooms will shrink during this time so push them down until they are covered with the oil. When they are cooked, pour off the oil that is above the level of the mushrooms. Keep it for later use: to flavour sauces or to add a wonderful taste to fried potatoes. Add the vinegar, and pour the mushrooms into sterilized jars. They will keep for at least a month, as long as you don't eat them before their time is up.

FRIED CEPS WITH GARLIC

Buledri frite incu l'agliu

One day we went to visit some American friends who had rented a villa across the bay. We hadn't announced our visit and they were out. As we were about to leave, I happened to glance into the garden of the house next door. It was covered with enormous ceps. The house itself was closely shuttered and looked as if it hadn't been lived in for a long time. Or at least that was what I told myself. 'It seems a shame,' I murmured to John. 'Yes, doesn't it?' he agreed. We filled the boot of the car and stole off like the thieves we were. As we finished our plates-full that evening we both assured each other that it would have been sinful to have left the ceps to rot and that the owner of the house would have been happy to see that they hadn't gone to waste. Here's how I cooked them.

Wipe the ceps with a damp cloth and pull out the stems. Chop the stems and cut the heads into thickish slices. Heat some olive oil in a frying-pan and fry the ceps over a medium heat for a few minutes, turning them over with a spatula. Add a handful of chopped parsley and some chopped cloves of garlic and salt and pepper to taste. Lower the heat and continue cooking, turning them frequently, for about 15 minutes. Eat them while they're hot.

POUTARGUE

Buttaraga

Poutargue is made from the roe of grey mullet, which is fished from the lagoons or *étangs* on the east coast: Diane, Urbino, Biguglia and Palo. It is fabricated between the beginning of July and thc end of September. Known as the caviar of Corsica, it is sought-after and very expensive, mainly because there is so little of it.

Poutargue has been enjoyed since Antiquity in Corsica. The roes of the fish are delicately removed and salted and pressed for several days before being rinsed, air-dried and lightly smoked. Usually served cut into very thin slices with bread and butter and lemon, it can also be crushed with olive oil, pepper and lemon juice.

L'ANCHOÏADE

I love picking the first green figs of the season in late spring and combining them with anchovies to make this unusual version of *anchoïade*.

8 whole salted anchovies or a small tin of anchovies in oil
1 large ripe green fig
2 cloves garlic
2 tbsp olive oil

If using salted anchovies you must wash them and prise the fillets off the bones. Peel the garlic. Mix the first three ingredients together in a mixer or pound in a mortar. Add a little oil if you are using salted anchovies. Brush toasted country-style bread slices with olive oil and spread with the *anchoïade*. This sauce is also delicious mixed with hot tagliatelle, the combination somehow tastes of the sea.

LEEK FRITTERS
Impurrate

These are lovely served as a starter to a meal or as a accompaniment to fish or meat.

4 large leeks
2 tbsp chopped mint
1 tbsp oil, salt and pepper
For the batter:
5 g dried yeast, pinch sugar
200g plain flour
1 tsp salt
1 egg
1 tbsp oil
about 300 ml water

To make the batter, mix the yeast and sugar in a small bowl with a little warm water and leave for 10 minutes to activate. Sieve the flour and salt into a bowl. Separate the egg and mix the yolk, together with the oil, into the flour. Gradually add enough water to make a batter the consistency of thick cream, stirring well to eliminate any lumps. Add the yeast mixture and mix well. Leave to rise, covered with a cloth, in a warm place for 2 hours or longer.

Meanwhile, split the leeks lengthways and wash them under running water. Slice thinly. Heat the oil in a frying-pan or saucepan and cook the leeks gently until they wilt slightly. Drain them in a colander and season well with salt and pepper. Mix in the chopped mint.

Beat the egg white with a pinch of salt until stiff and fold into the batter together with the leeks. Drop spoonfuls of the mixture into a deep fryer of medium hot oil and cook until golden brown, turning each fritter over halfway through the cooking time. Drain each batch on kitchen paper and keep them warm in a low oven until you have cooked them all.

Using the same batter, you can make herb fritters. Traditionally, these are made with nine different plants: mint, camomile leaves, dandelion leaves, wild chard, parsley, wild garlic, spring onions and *népète* or *népéta* (Latin *nepeta*, in English calamint) which tastes like a mixture of oregano and mint. You can however make very tasty fritters using just spring onions, mint, parsley or basil and a few leaves of spinach or Swiss chard. Allow about 500 grams of mixed plants to the above batter. Wash and finely chop the plants and herbs and squeeze them dry in a clean teacloth or kitchen paper (very important). Mix them with the batter and fry as above.

BROCCIU AND ANCHOVY TARTS

Torta incu anchiuve e brocciu

For the pastry:
8 anchovy fillets
250 g plain flour
5 tbsp olive oil
2 eggs
For the filling:
150 g fresh brocciu
12 anchovy fillets

Chop the anchovies. Rub the oil into the flour, add 1 egg and the chopped anchovies. Form into a ball and leave for 1 hour wrapped in aluminium foil. Roll the pastry out thinly and cut into squares or circles. Put slices of *brocciu* and anchovy fillet on half of them. Wet the edges of the pastry and cover with the other pieces, pinching the edges together well to seal them. Separate the second egg and brush the tops of the pastry with the yolk. Bake the tarts in a preheated moderate oven (200°C/gas 6) until golden.

BROCCIU AND MINT OMELETTE

Frittata incu brocciu Serves 3 to 4

Omelettes in Corsica are cooked with oil, not butter, and are not folded over in the same way as French omelettes, but cooked flat. They are, however, served while still juicy.

12 mint leaves
100 g brocciu
6 eggs
salt and pepper
olive oil

Chop the mint leaves. Crush the *brocciu* roughly with a fork. Beat the eggs, season with salt and pepper and add the mint and cheese. Heat the oil in a frying-pan and tip in the eggs. As the egg mixture sets move it from the sides into the centre so that the uncooked egg runs underneath. While the omelette is still runny put a plate over the pan and invert the omelette onto it. Slide the omelette back into the pan, runny side down, and cook for a few seconds. Serve with the least cooked side uppermost.

COURGETTE AND POTATO OMELETTE

Frittata incu zucchine e pommi Serves 3 to 4

2 courgettes
2 potatoes
6 eggs
salt and pepper
olive oil

Finely dice the courgettes and peel and dice the potatoes. Heat a little olive oil in a frying-pan and cook the potatoes for 5 minutes, turning them often. Add the courgettes and continue cooking. Beat the eggs together and season with salt and pepper. When the potatoes are tender tip in the eggs and cook the omelette as in the preceding recipe.

EGGS WITH TOMATOES

Ovi incu a pumata Serves 3

There are a lot of variations on the following recipe. Sometimes the eggs are beaten together with the sauce and cooked like a *frittata* instead of being cooked whole. The *panzetta* is optional, as is the hot red chilli pepper. Sometimes grated cheese is sprinkled over the top at the moment of serving.

100 g cubed panzetta
1 onion, chopped
1 hot red chilli pepper, deseeded and chopped
1 chopped clove garlic
3 large or 5 medium tomatoes, skinned, seeded and chopped (or tinned)
1 bay leaf or 1 tbsp chopped basil
olive oil
salt and pepper
3 to 6 eggs

Heat the oil in a large frying-pan and cook the cubed *panzetta* over a fairly high heat until it starts to brown. Lower the heat and add the onion and chilli pepper. Cook until the onion softens and add the garlic, chopped tomatoes, herbs and seasonings. Stir well and simmer for about 10 minutes. Break one or two eggs on top for each person and continue cooking until the eggs are set.

HERB TART

Torta incu l'erba

This is an absolutely delicious tart that I serve with a salad for a light lunch or as a beginning for a more substantial meal. Make sure that there is plenty of filling as it will shrink a bit when it is baked. If you're in a hurry, you can use ready-made shortcrust or puff pastry.

For the pastry:
80 g lard or 125 g butter
250 g plain flour
pinch salt
For the filling:
1 kilo Swiss chard or spinach, or a mixture
3 leeks
1 onion or a bunch of spring onions
1 tbsp chopped basil or mint
1 tsp népéta, *or marjoram*
1 tbsp olive oil, salt and pepper
1 egg yolk for brushing pastry and 1 egg (optional)

Rub the butter or lard into the flour and salt with your fingertips and add just enough water to hold the pastry together. Wrap in foil and leave to rest for 30 minutes. Remove the stems of the chard and/or spinach and wash the leaves well. Cook in a small amount of salted water for 5 minutes. Drain well, pressing in a sieve or cloth to remove all liquid. Split and wash the leeks and slice very thinly. Finely chop the onions including the green parts if using spring onions. Heat the oil in a frying-pan and cook the onions and leeks gently until they wilt. Chop the chard and spinach and mix with the onions, leeks and herbs. Season well. Roll out a little over half the pastry and line the bottom of a tart dish. Fill with the greens and roll out the rest of the pastry to make a lid. Seal the edges by pinching them together and brush over the pastry with the egg yolk. Make a small hole in the centre of the tart and put in a little roll of cardboard or tinfoil to make a funnel. Cook in a preheated oven (220°C/ gas 7) for 25 to 30 minutes. Serve warm. Sometimes a beaten egg or some cream is added to the vegetables before filling the pie.

SWISS CHARD AND BROCCIU TURNOVERS

Bastelle Makes 5

These puff pastry turnovers are a speciality of Ajaccio and are sold in the market as well as in most bakery shops. They can be made with the pastry used in the preceding recipe.

300 g puff pastry
1 bunch Swiss chard
200 g brocciu *or cream cheese*
salt and pepper

Remove the thick white stems of the chard and use for another dish. Wash the leaves and cook in a little salted water for 5 minutes. Drain and cool and squeeze out any water in a sieve or cloth. Chop and season well. Roll out the pastry and cut into 6 squares or circles (use a saucer as a guide). Put a portion of chard and *brocciu* on each piece of pastry and fold in half. Brush the edges with a little water and pinch together. Either deep-fry until a golden brown or bake in a preheated oven (200°C/gas 6) for about 25 minutes.

The turnovers are also sold filled with sliced onions which have been cooked very slowly in oil, or pumpkin which has been cooked in a little oil and highly seasoned with pepper. When *brocciu* is not in season they are made with Swiss chard only.

SNAILS

When Charlie was about two and a half, a lady in the fish market gave her one of the snails she was selling for her to keep as a pet. We put it in a shoe box, fed it on lettuce leaves, and called it Fred. It grew very large and turned green. Charlie spent hours chatting to it and patting its shell so that when John declared he had an irresistible urge to eat snails à la bourguignonne, I decided we might have a problem on our hands. John assured me that he didn't want to eat Fred and would be more than happy with snails already stuffed with garlic butter in their shells. Nevertheless we thought we'd wait until Charlie was tucked up for the night before tucking in ourselves.

We were half way through our feast and mopping up the delicious juices with bread when I became aware of a small pyjama-clad figure standing beside the table, saying something and staring at us accusingly. I guiltily tried to cover up my plate fearing she was about to become traumatized for life. To my concern she burst into tears and through her sobs repeated the same phrase until, utterly frustrated by our incomprehension, she stamped her foot and yelled, 'I want Freds!' So the three of us finished them up.

In Corsica snails are often served in a wine and tomato sauce. It is usual to gather your own snails and then to purge them for a several days before cooking them. A good way to do this is to put them in an empty plastic mineral water bottle, in which you have made several holes. Cover the top so that they can't escape and leave them for four or five days.

A quicker method is to soak them in a vinegar and water mixture. Using rubber gloves, gather a big bunch of nettles at the same time as you hunt for snails. Almost fill a large bowl with cold water and add a bottle of vinegar. Put in the snails and the nettles and mix well every 20 minutes for two hours. Remove the nettles and whatever is clinging to them. Rinse the snails very well four or five times in running water.

Cook them in a pot of simmering salted water with an added bay leaf, for 30 to 40 minutes.

Of course, if the spirit of adventure is lacking, or you simply don't have the time, you can always buy them already cleaned and pre-cooked in tins, which is what I usually do.

SNAILS IN WINE SAUCE

Lumaca incu vinu Serves 4 to 6

1 tin of snails (about 8 dozen small snails)
2 shallots, finely chopped
2 cloves garlic, crushed and chopped
1 or 2 hot red chillis, or 8 anchovy fillets
1 tbsp tomato concentrate
½ a bottle of red wine
2 bay leaves, 1 sprig thyme, 1 sprig rosemary
500 ml veal or chicken stock

Heat 2 tablespoons of oil in a saucepan and gently cook the shallots and garlic until soft. Stir in the tomato, herbs, and chillis (or anchovy fillets) and add the wine and stock. Bring to the boil, lower the heat, and simmer until the sauce is reduced by half. Remove the chillis and season to taste. Add the drained snails and divide between 4 or 6 small heat-proof dishes. Put in a hot oven (225°C/gas 8) for 5 minutes and serve with lots of crusty bread to soak up the juices.

FISH AND SHELLFISH

Corsicans were traditionally mountain-dwellers, living in their strong granite houses in villages clinging to the hillsides, safe from the marauding pirates who, for centuries, attacked the coastline, razing houses to the ground, enslaving any unfortunate souls they happened to find. Those who did venture down to the coast with their flocks of sheep and goats also faced the dangers of malaria which infected most of the coastline of Corsica up until the end of the Second World War.

Until then, fishing had been mainly centred in the very north and south of the island and around the two main towns, Ajaccio and Bastia. Now, the hundred kilometres of coastline is exploited by about 350 professional fishermen. Their small wooden boats (rarely longer than 10 metres) known as *pointus* usually keep to a limit of six sea-miles. Their catch may consist of red mullet, John Dory, scorpion fish, sea bream, *mustelle*, conger eel, octopus, weaver fish, sardines, anchovies and, in season, lobster, spider crab and, the prize of them all, *langouste*, the spiny crawfish of which all Corsicans are inordinately fond. A few larger boats fish up to the ten-mile limit for tuna, swordfish, sharks, rays and angler fish.

On the east coast of the island are the oyster and mussel farms. The large lagoons which run into the sea are fished from flat-bottomed boats for bream, bass, eels, cuttlefish and spider crabs.

INTERLUDE: A STORM AND A FEAST

The bright yellow Genoa sail billowed out and John, hanging on to the halyards, tried to sit in it. It was a glorious blustery day of brilliant sunshine and *Ratu Etai*, our catamaran, was sailing at seven knots, an all-time record. We were headed for the islands of Lavezzi some seven sea-miles south of Corsica in the Strait of Bonifacio. Half an hour later we rounded the southernmost tip of the islands and changed tack to bring the boat back into the sheltered bay tucked into the western corner. It was completely calm and, as we anchored, we marvelled that we were the only people there. The Lavezzi islands are uninhabited apart from a guardian and his dog, who allegedly live there. We had never seen them but had heard that Brigitte Bardot had once captured the dog supposing it to be abandoned.

Rob, an Australian friend who was sailing with us, dived overboard and swam ashore while John and I unlashed the dinghy to take Charlie, our five-year-old daughter, to the beach, which is one of the prettiest that I know. At either end it is made up of minuscule but perfect shells. Just behind it is the cemetery of the crew and passengers of the ill-fated frigate *The Semillante*. This sank in a storm in 1855 en route for the Crimea with the loss of all 750 people aboard. Of these, 580 bodies were recovered, including that of the captain, identified by his club-foot. It is a very simple and beautiful resting place.

Some people say the islands are haunted and that at night you can hear the wailing of ghosts. In fact, when the wind blows through the great holes in the granite rocks which stand all over the island, it does make a noise which sounds very much like wailing, and we fell asleep that night listening to it.

When we tuned into the weather forecast the next day we heard that the blusters of the day before had turned to a full-blown storm. With the evidence of what a storm in the

Bonifacio straits could wreak lying before us in the cemetery, we decided to stay put.

Three days later the storm was still raging. We had swum, fished and sunbathed. John and Rob had cleaned the sides of the boat and I had baked bread. No other boats had arrived, nor were likely to in the storm. We decided to explore the other side of the island. Feeling very Robinson Crusoeish, we left Tiggypuss the cat in charge of *Ratu Etai* (hoping Brigitte Bardot wouldn't find her alone) and set off across the sparsely vegetated land behind the beach. We came across enormous pillars of granite lying on the ground and John remembered being told stories of ancient granite quarries on the islands.

We soon reached the bay on the other side. It was fairly well protected but, beyond it, we could see the full fury of the storm and were thankful to be in so safe an anchorage. As we neared the water, I saw that the bottom of the bay was almost black and realized that it was covered with sea urchins. Moreover, they almost all had something adhering to them, a shell, a small pebble or a piece of seaweed. This is one way of telling that they are good to eat. The inedible black variety is always naked of adornment. Rob willingly went back to the boat to fetch bags and long spoons to prise them off their hold on the rocks and before long we had as many as we could carry.

In the cockpit of *Ratu Etai*, armed with three pairs of scissors, we dug the points into the core of each sea urchin and cut around the tops. Then we shook the urchins upside down over the side of the boat. We were left with the corals, the orange-coloured segments, which we scooped out with crusty pieces of bread. They tasted salty-sweet and had a texture a bit like peach flesh. Delicious, especially with a glass of cold white wine. We ate until we could eat no more, swinging our legs over the limpid, crystal-clear water, watching the fish darting about snatching the breadcrumbs that fell from our fingers.

When we had finished, we still had several sea urchins left. I scooped out the corals and folded them into a mayonnaise, which I poured over sliced hard-boiled eggs. We called the dish Eggs Lavezzi. A few months later, we were visiting an English friend on holiday in Corsica. She was staying in an hotel by the sea, on the road between Ajaccio and the Îles Sanguinaires. The owner of the hotel, a keen diver, had decided to give his guests a treat and was on the terrace of his hotel, still in his diving suit, serving them freshly-gathered sea urchins and white wine. 'Well,' said a loud feminine English voice, 'if they'll eat that, they'll eat anything.' You betcha!

If, on a self-catering, camping or yachting holiday, you are lucky enough to find some sea urchins, here are some recipes for cooking them. Of course, nothing can beat eating them 'au nature' beside the sea, but they're also delicious cooked. *Oursinade* is the name for a feast of sea urchins and *oursinado* is the name of the following dish.

OURSINADO

Serves 6

3 dozen sea urchins
2 medium or 1 large chopped onion
1 chopped carrot
half a bottle of dry white wine
4 sprigs parsley, 1sprig thyme, 1 bay leaf
1 1/2 kilos of cleaned white fish cut into thick slices. Choose a mixture of three or four of the following: angler fish, sea bream, bass, cod, hake, haddock, halibut or turbot
100 g butter
6 egg yolks
salt and pepper
6 slices of day-old French bread, toasted

Open the sea urchins with a pair of scissors or with a special cutter. Put the corals into a small bowl and keep cool. Put the carrot and onions into a big saucepan with the white wine, herbs and salt and pepper. Bring to the boil and simmer for 10 minutes. Add the fish and, if necessary, water to cover. Bring to the boil again, lower the heat and simmer for about 10 minutes, until the fish is just cooked. Remove the fish and keep warm. Meanwhile melt the butter in a bowl over a saucepan of boiling water and stir in the egg yolks. Add two ladles of the liquid from the fish to the bowl and beat all together until creamy. Add the corals to this mixture and stir well. Correct the seasoning. Put the toast into a serving dish and moisten well with the fish stock. Pour over the sea urchin sauce and serve together with the pieces of fish.

Sea urchins can be folded into a hollandaise or mousseline sauce to serve with steamed or baked fish.

HOLLANDAISE SAUCE

4 egg yolks
2 tbsp cold water
125 g softened butter
1 tbsp lemon juice
salt and white pepper

Put the egg yolks, water and salt and pepper in a bowl set over a saucepan of hot, not boiling, water. Whisk until the mixture thickens and then draw the pan to one side. Gradually add the butter in little pieces, whisking all the time. Add the lemon juice. The sauce must not boil or it will curdle. To make mousseline sauce, add some whipped cream to warm, not hot, hollandaise.

SEA URCHIN SOUFFLÉ

I zini suffiate

Serves 4

2 dozen sea urchins
4 eggs plus 2 whites
35 g butter
35 g plain flour
150 ml full-cream milk
salt and pepper

Prepare a soufflé dish by buttering or oiling it. Cut a round of greaseproof paper to fit the bottom and put it in place. Tie a double band of greaseproof paper around the dish so that it stands 6 centimetres above the top, to protect the soufflé as it rises.

Cut open the sea urchins with a pair of scissors and remove and save the corals. If you prefer to cook the soufflé in the shells, save twelve of the neatest and wash them well before buttering the insides.

Separate the eggs. Melt the butter in a pan and stir in the flour. Cook for a minute or two, stirring all the while and gradually stir in the milk, incorporating it as you go along. Bring to the boil and then simmer, still stirring, for a few minutes. Take off the heat and cool slightly before beating in the egg yolks, one by one. Season with salt and pepper and cool a little before stirring in the sea urchin corals. Beat the egg whites until very stiff and fold into the sea urchin mixture. Pile into the prepared soufflé dish and cook in a preheated oven (180°C/gas 4) for about 30 minutes, until well risen and golden. Alternatively, fill the buttered shells and cook for 10 minutes.

SEA URCHINS WITH EGGS

I zini incu u ovi

Serves 4

Sea urchins are also good folded into creamy scrambled eggs at the last minute of cooking, or as a filling for a buttery omelette.

Here is another way of preparing sea urchins which is particularly useful if you only have a few. Allow three per serving.

12 sea urchins
200 ml single cream
12 quail eggs
salt and pepper

Carefully open the urchins and, with a teaspoon, remove the corals. Reserve. Clean the insides of the shells and remove any loose spines. Pour a tablespoon of cream into each shell and carefully break an egg on top. The best way to do this is to make a small cut with a sharp knife in the shell and break the egg into a small saucer. Slide it into the sea urchin shell and arrange the corals on top. Season lightly with salt and pepper. Arrange the sea urchins in a baking dish and cook in a preheated oven (220°C/gas 7) for 5 minutes. This really brings out the taste of the sea urchins.

BOUILLABAISSE

Aziminu Serves 6 to 8

The most famous of all Mediterranean dishes, this was originally a simple one-pot meal cooked by the fishermen themselves.

2 kilos mixed fish and shellfish (mussels, queens, and the like), including rascasse *(scorpion fish), some little rock fish for the sauce and some pieces of moray or conger eel for their firm flesh. Other fish could include grouper, sea bass, weaver, bream etc.*
2 onions, sliced
3 cloves garlic, crushed
1 fennel bulb, sliced (optional)
2 tbsp tomato concentrate
½ tsp saffron
1 bay leaf, 3 sprigs thyme
a few small or one medium peeled potato per person
olive oil, salt and pepper

If you can, persuade the fishmonger to clean and scale the fish for you. If you do it yourself be careful with the *rascasse* as the spines are very sharp. The weaver will usually have had its spines already removed. Heat some oil in a large saucepan and start cooking the onions, garlic and fennel (if you are using it). Add the small fish and any little shellfish that there may be, crushing them down with the back of a wooden spoon. Stir in the tomato paste, saffron and herbs. Put in the peeled potatoes, cutting larger ones into thick slices. Add 2 litres water, seasonings and bring to the boil.

Add the slices of eel, bring back to the boil again and add the other fish, putting in the thickest first. Lower the heat and continue cooking for 10 minutes. Serve the broth first with some potatoes for each serving, toasted bread, *rouille* and cloves of garlic. Guests rub their toast with a cut clove of garlic and put it in the soup. Put the fish on a serving dish surrounded with the rest of the potatoes and some liquid. Leftovers can be turned into soup.

A more refined version of this stew would have you (after adding the small fish and shellfish, tomato, saffron and herbs) add 1/2 litre of water, salt and pepper and bring to the boil. Lower the heat and simmer for 30 minutes. Put this through a food mill or press through a sieve, pushing through as much of the solids as possible. Reheat this sauce with the rest of the water until boiling and add the slices of eel and potatoes. Simmer for ten minutes and add the other fish, putting in the largest first. Bring to the boil again, lower heat and simmer for another 10 minutes or until the flesh in the thickest fish just comes away from the backbone when pushed with a knife. Serve as above.

ROUILLE, MARK TWO

There is a bread-based *rouille* given with the fish soup on page 42. If you prefer, here is a mayonnaise-based one.

1/2 cup mayonnaise
2 cloves of garlic, crushed and chopped
1 tsp hot pimentón or cayenne pepper or 1 tbsp chilli pepper purée or sambal olek

Blend all the ingredients together or pound the garlic and pepper together in a mortar and add to the mayonnaise.

BOUILLABAISSE OF SALT COD

Aziminu di baccala Serves 6

Salt cod is popular in most Mediterranean countries. Salting has been a way of preserving food for centuries. Before using the fish it must be soaked in cold water that is changed often, for times varying between 12 and 48 hours. The kite-shaped salted and dried cod takes the longest time and the fillets of cod that are just salted take about 12 hours.

1 kilo salt cod soaked for the appropriate time
2 tbsp olive oil
2 onions, sliced
4 cloves garlic, crushed
1/2 bulb fennel, sliced
2 tbsp tomato concentrate or 4 ripe tomatoes, peeled and chopped
1 piece of orange peel (optional)
6 potatoes, peeled and sliced
pinch of saffron
1 bay leaf, 2 sprigs thyme
salt and pepper

Skin and bone the cod and cut it into squares. Heat the oil and gently fry the onion until it wilts. Add the garlic, fennel and tomato and cook, stirring, for a minute. Add the rest of the ingredients (except for the cod) and a litre of cold water. Bring to the boil, reduce heat and simmer for 30 minutes. Add the cod and cook for 10 minutes more. Serve with *rouille*, toasted country bread and some garlic cloves to rub it with.

BOUILLABAISSE OF EGGS

Aziminu di ovi

Make the bouillabaisse as above and replace the cod with eggs, which you poach in the broth. If you are nervous about poaching the eggs you could substitute peeled soft-boiled eggs. Serve the eggs on toasted buttered bread, surround with the potatoes and pour the broth over the top. Serve with aiöli or *rouille* sauce.

SALT COD AND LEEKS

Baccala incu porri

When a Corsican cries 'Baccala per Corsica' he is implying that he is being cheated. The dictum translates as 'Salt cod for Corsicans' and refers to the way the inferior salt cod that was sent to the Corsicans by the Genoese was labelled. Salt cod often replaced fresh fish in the mountain areas and was stewed, baked or prepared in fritters. It was eaten on days of fasting and is still served on the Friday before All Saints' Day with leeks, Swiss chard or chickpeas.

1 kilo salt cod soaked in cold water for the appropriate time (see page 70)
2 tbsp olive oil
1 kilo leeks
2 tbsp tomato concentrate
1 tbsp plain flour
1 bay leaf
pepper
½ litre water

Remove skin and bones from the salt cod and cut into squares. Heat the oil in a wide saucepan and fry the pieces of cod until lightly coloured. Remove and set aside. Clean and slice the leeks. Fry them gently in the oil until they soften. Add the tomato concentrate, flour, pepper and bay leaf. Stir for a minute or two and then add the water. Simmer for 20 minutes. Add the cod and simmer for 10 more minutes.

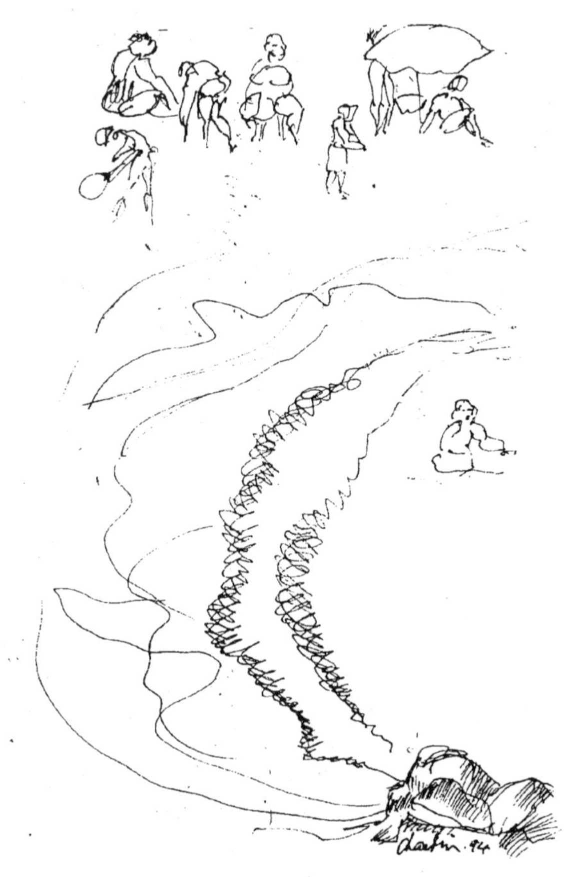

SALT COD WITH SWISS CHARD AND RAISINS

U baccala incu e biettule Serves 4

This is a dish from the town of Bonifacio on the southernmost tip of the island where cooking was influenced by invasions of the Moors and the Spanish during the Middle Ages. The sweet and sour combination of tastes works very well.

600 g salted cod
1 bunch Swiss chard
1 onion
2 cloves garlic
2 tomatoes, peeled, seeded and chopped
4 potatoes, peeled and quartered
2 tbsp chopped parsley
1 bay leaf
4 tbsp raisins
salt and pepper

Soak the cod in cold water for the appropriate time (see page 70). Take out any bones and cut into medium pieces. Wash the Swiss chard and cut out the white stems. Save these for another dish. Cook the leaves in a little salted water for 5 minutes. Drain well and chop. Reserve. Chop the onion and garlic and cook in a little olive oil until beginning to go soft. Add the tomatoes, potatoes, parsley, pepper and bay leaf and just enough water to cover. Bring to the boil, lower the heat and simmer for 20 minutes. Add the cod, raisins and Swiss chard and continue cooking for 10 minutes. Add salt if needed and serve hot in wide soup bowls.

SQUID IN TOMATO SAUCE

Totani incu a pumata Serves 6

Calamar or squid must be cooked either very quickly or for at least an hour; anything in between will render it tough. Nowadays, we tend to favour the quick method but traditional Mediterranean cooking involves long simmering, which has the advantage of impregnating the squid with the flavour of the sauce in which it has been cooked.

1 kilo cleaned squid
1 large onion
2 cloves garlic
5 ripe tomatoes
1 hot red chilli pepper, deseeded or 1/2 tsp cayenne pepper
2 sprigs thyme, 1 bay leaf
salt and pepper
olive oil

If they are not already prepared, remove the plastic-like cartilage from the insides of the squid and pull the bodies from the tentacles, throwing away the beak and head. Remove the soft insides and discard. Rub off the outside skin. Cut the bodies of the squid into rings and chop the tentacles. Peel and chop the onion and garlic. Skin and chop the tomatoes. Heat some oil in a saucepan and fry the onion over a low heat for one or two minutes. Add the squid and cook for a few minutes, stirring, with the onion. Add the garlic and herbs and chilli pepper or cayenne and then the tomatoes. Season well and simmer, covered, for one hour. Remove the chilli pepper and serve the squid with rice.

STUFFED SQUID IN CRAB SAUCE

Totani a modu bastaise Serves 6

For the crab sauce:
3 tbsp olive oil
*175 g fresh or frozen crab meat (including brown meat) or 500 g small, live velvet crabs (*Étrilles*)*
1 chopped onion
1 red chilli pepper
1 bay leaf, 2 sprigs thyme
3 tbsp brandy
5 ripe tomatoes, chopped or 1 tin chopped tomatoes
1/2 bottle dry white wine
1 tbsp chopped mint or oregano (or nepita)
salt and pepper
For the squid:
1 kilo squid
300 g minced pork or chopped ham
2 cloves garlic, finely chopped
2 tbsp chopped parsley
200 g fresh breadcrumbs
1 egg, salt and pepper

First make the sauce. Heat the oil in a saucepan and put in the crabs. (If you are using ready-prepared crab meat, add it at the end.) When the crabs turn red, break them up with the back of a wooden spoon and add the chopped onion, chilli pepper and herbs. Cook for a few minutes until the onion starts to soften. Flame with the brandy and then add the tomatoes. Cook for a minute or two and add the white wine. Season well and bring to the boil. Lower heat and simmer, covered, for 30 minutes. Put through a food mill. If you are using ready-prepared crab, add it now.

Clean the squid as in the preceding recipe. Rinse the bodies and set aside. Chop the tentacles finely and mix with the other ingredients. Season well. Using a teaspoon, fill the bodies (not too full) and fasten each of them with a toothpick. Cook them in the crab sauce for about 30 minutes or until tender. Test with a fork: when it pierces the squid easily, they are cooked. If the sauce seems to be drying out during cooking, add a little hot water. Serve with rice.

You can cook the squid in a plain tomato sauce if you prefer and you could replace the meat in the stuffing with anchovies, just as you can substitute a little cooked rice for the breadcrumbs.

OCTOPUS WITH POTATOES

U polpu incu i pommi Serves 6

Octopus are fished and eaten all over the Mediterranean. On the island of Elba, I've eaten it cooked and sold from a big pot on the corner of a street. From my window overlooking the fishermen's port in Ajaccio, I often see small boys triumphantly bearing off the octopus that they have just speared. Maybe their mothers cook it the following way.

1 kilo prepared and tenderized octopus
2 tbsp olive oil
1 onion, chopped
2 cloves garlic, crushed
3 tomatoes, peeled and chopped
salt and pepper
1 kilo potatoes, peeled and cut into thick slices
2 tbsp chopped parsley

Cut the octopus into pieces and gently fry in the oil together with the onion, until the onion starts to soften. Add the garlic and tomatoes and stir for a minute or two. Season with salt and pepper, cover with water. Bring to the boil and then simmer for one hour. Add the potatoes and parsley and continue cooking for 30 minutes.

ESCABECHE
Scabecciu

Escabeche is a form of preserved fish found all over the Mediterranean. The following version comes from the north of Corsica and uses myrtle berries which grow in profusion in the *maquis*, the densc undergrowth of all sorts of different shrubs and trees which covers over one-fifth of the island's surface. Myrtle berries were often used in place of pepper in traditional recipes, particularly with game dishes, as well as being made into a strong liqueur, drunk as a *digestif* at the end of a meal. Free-range cows and various game also feed on the berries: they give their flesh a special flavour.

1 kilo mackerel or other oily fish
salt and pepper, flour
300 ml olive oil
1 lemon
100 g myrtle berries
2 bay leaves
2 crushed cloves garlic
150 ml wine vinegar
50 ml water

Behead and gut the mackerel. Put some flour and seasoning into a plastic bag. Put the fish in the bag one at a time and shake them so that they are well coated. Fry them in 100 ml of hot oil for 4 minutes on each side. Put them into an oven dish just large enough to hold them side by side. Cut the lemon in thin slices and spread over the fish. Clean the frying-pan and heat the rest of the oil. Add the myrtle berries, bay leaves and garlic. Cook for one minute and add the vinegar and water. Season and simmer for 5 minutes. Pour over the fish and leave to cool. Chill in the fridge and serve cold. This dish can be kept for several days in the fridge.

EELS WITH WILD CHICORY

Anguille incu a lattaredda

Eels are highly appreciated in Corsica. They can be found in most of the rivers and lakes and especially in the great lagoon or *étang* of Biguglia, south of Bastia on the east coast. Since the sixteenth century, and probably before, they were exported live to Naples and Rome, particularly for the festivals of Holy Week and for Christmas. Wild chicory (*lattaredda* or *lattarepulu*) is the most commonly used wild herb in Corsica, either mixed with other herbs in a tart or soup or, as here, used to give a refreshing, slightly sour taste to counterbalance the richness of the eels. Failing a supply of the wild herb, you can make do with a mixture of spinach and sorrel.

1 kilo eels
3 bunches (250 g) wild chicory
200 ml dry white wine
1 onion
2 cloves garlic
1 bay leaf, 2 sprigs thyme, 2 sprigs rosemary
6 tbsp olive oil
2 tbsp plain flour
salt and pepper
200 ml water

Kill, gut and skin the eels and cut into thick slices. Easier said than done (I speak from experience as my brother, a keen fisherman, would bring me buckets of these wiggling things when he lived in Corsica). Eels should be alive until just before you cook them. You will need two cloths, one to hold the eel and one to hold the skin. You will also need something heavy to bash the eel on the head and a sharp pointed knife to behead it. Do not be disconcerted if it leaps around a bit after it is headless – it's just nerves. The most difficult bit is skinning the thing. Cut away a corner of the skin at the top end. Use some sea salt and a cloth to hold the skin and peel it off like a stocking. You may have to hold down the rest of the eel with a large fork. Cut the eel into thick slices and rinse well. (It's useful to know that small eels don't need to be skinned.)

Remove the stalks from the chicory and blanch the leaves for one minute in boiling salted water. Drain, chop coarsely and keep aside. Heat 3 tbsp of the oil in a saucepan and fry the onions over a low heat until they begin to soften. Add the heads of the eels, the garlic and herbs and the wine and water. Season with salt and pepper and bring to the boil. Lower heat, cover and simmer for 30 minutes. Put in the pieces of eel and cook over a low heat for 20 minutes. Remove the eel and keep warm. Heat the rest of the oil (or butter) in another pan and stir in the flour. Gradually strain in the liquid, stirring well to remove any lumps. Put the chicory in the bottom of a greased oven dish and lay the pieces of eel on top. Pour the sauce over the eels and chicory and bake in a preheated oven (200°C/gas 6) for 10 minutes.

LANGOUSTE WITH SPAGHETTI AND TWO SAUCES

Aligosta incu spaghetti Serves 4

1 large, 2 medium or 4 small langoustes *(weighing in total about 1 ½ kilos)*
salt

Langouste (spiny lobster or crawfish) is the prize of all shellfish in Corsica, eaten on high days and holidays. You can substitute lobster or crab if crawfish are unobtainable. There are many recommended ways of killing shellfish humanely, and an interesting discussion of the question can be found in Alan Davidson's *Mediterranean Seafood*. Crabs do need dispatching with an awl before being placed in boiling water. Lobsters and crawfish can also be quickly dealt with by a blow of the knife if boiling is not the chosen cooking method but, if it is, a routine I was always advised to follow was to put the chosen shellfish in a saucepan of warm salty water and bring to the boil. It should go to sleep thinking it's in a rock pool, but keep a lid on it just in case. The RSPCA currently advise that the shellfish should be rendered unconscious by being put in a freezer for some time before boiling. A further trick I have been told is to hold the *langouste* on its back and stroke it firmly down its front. It will become unconscious. (A friend of mine says it would have the opposite effect on *him*.) Once these preliminaries have been observed and the fish is in the boiling water, lower the heat and cook for about 20 minutes. Take the lid off and let the shellfish cool in the water. Remove it and save the water to cook the spaghetti.

Make a fresh tomato sauce as follows:

3 slices coppa *(cured pork tenderloin) or 1 slice* prizuttu *or cured ham, diced small (optional)*
1 onion, chopped
2 cloves garlic, chopped
1 tbsp tomato concentrate
1 kilo ripe tomatoes, peeled and chopped or 1 large tin chopped tomatoes
1 bay leaf, 2 sprigs thyme
olive oil, salt and pepper

Heat a little oil in a saucepan and gently fry the *coppa* or ham. Add the onion and garlic and cook until soft. Stir in the tomato paste and add the tomatoes, herbs and salt and pepper to taste. Cook over a low heat for 30 minutes.

Split the *langouste* or lobster down the centre and take out the liver and coral. Discard the stomach sac (between the eyes) and feathery gills. Cut the tail meat in slices and replace in the shells. Crack the claws and keep the shellfish warm in a very low oven. If you are using a crab, open the shell from the back and take out all the dark meat. Put in a bowl. Pick out the white meat carefully from the centre section and the claws, making sure there are no bits of shell. Put into another bowl.

Make a second sauce of the corals as follows:

2 shallots, very finely chopped
2 tbsp butter
the liver (tomally) and coral of the shellfish (or dark crab meat)
100 ml double cream
1 tbsp cognac
salt, pinch of cayenne pepper

Cook the shallots in the butter until soft. Stir in the tomally and coral (or dark meat) mashing it with a fork, and add the cream and cognac. Season with salt and cayenne.

Taste the shellfish water for saltiness, add more water if necessary, and cook the spaghetti in it. Drain and toss with the tomato sauce. Pour the cream sauce over the crawfish and serve on top of the spaghetti. If you use crab, mix the tomato sauce, white meat and spaghetti together and serve the cream sauce apart.

LANGOUSTE AND POTATOES

Aligosta incu pommi Serves 4

This is a very old recipe from the north of the island. You could replace the crawfish with lobster. However, I am afraid you must cut the shellfish up alive. Turn them on to their fronts on a carving board and flatten them out with your hand. With a large, heavy knife separate the body from the head. Cut the tail into sections. Do not remove the shell as it will protect the flesh and flavour it during cooking. Put the pieces into a bowl. Cut the heads in half lengthways, remove and discard the stomach sac (between the eyes) and gills. Save the greeny-grey tomally and blackish roe (if it's a female) and any juices which may have leaked out.

1/3 wine glass olive oil
1 large, 2 medium or 4 small langoustes *(weighing in total about 1 1/2 kilos)*
2 tbsp eau de vie *or brandy*
1 large onion, finely chopped
6 ripe tomatoes skinned, seeded and chopped (or 1 tin chopped tomatoes)
3 cloves garlic, crushed
1 bay leaf, 2 sprigs thyme, 1 tbsp chopped parsley or basil
800 g firm potatoes
salt and pepper

Heat the oil in a wide pan and cook the pieces of crawfish until the shells redden all over. Take them out and reserve. Lower the heat and put in the cleaned head shells. Cook until they redden, then flame them with *eau de vie*. Add the onions and cook, stirring from time to time, for 3 minutes. Add the tomatoes, garlic and herbs and just enough water to cover. Bring to the boil, lower heat and simmer for about 20 to 30 minutes or until the sauce thickens. Remove the shells, bay leaf and thyme and put the sauce through either a food mill or blender. Clean the pan and return the sauce, seasoning to taste. Peel the potatoes and cut into thin slices. Cook in the sauce for 10 minutes. Add the tail pieces and cook, turning them from time to time, for 5 more minutes.

To serve, pile the tails in the middle of a large heated serving dish, surrounded by the potatoes. Take the sauce off the heat and whisk in the tomally, juices and roe. Rectify the seasoning and pour over and around the potatoes.

LANGOUSTE GRATIN

Aligosta u brocciu Serves 4

This method of serving *langouste* comes from Calvi, an old fishing port which is now a popular tourist town, on the north-west coast of Corsica and, incidentally, where Admiral Lord Nelson lost his eye in battle.

1 large or 2 medium langoustes *or lobsters (weighing in total about 1 1/2 kilos)*
150 g hard cheese (preferably Corsican or Italian)
2 egg yolks
2 tbsp olive oil
pepper
For the *court-bouillon*:
1 bay leaf, 2 sprigs thyme, 2 sprigs parsley
300 ml white wine
1 sliced carrot
1 sliced onion
salt and pepper
water (enough to cover the shellfish)

Put all the ingredients for the *court-bouillon* into a large saucepan and bring to a boil. Skim off any froth and simmer for 10 minutes. With the liquid still bubbling, put in the *langouste* head-first. It will die instantly. Simmer for 15 to 20 minutes, depending on size. Drain and cool. Split in half lengthways and remove the tail meat. Crack the claws and remove meat. Discard the stomach sac and feathery gills.

If the cheese is very salty, soak it for a couple of hours in cold water. Pat it dry and grate it. Pour two soup ladles of the bouillon into a saucepan and melt the cheese in it, stirring carefully. When the cheese has melted beat in the egg yolks and olive oil. Add salt, if needed, and pepper. Do not boil the sauce once you have added the yolks. Cut the shellfish meat into large slices, mix with the sauce and put back into the shells. Put them into a baking dish and cook in a medium-hot oven (220°C/gas 7) for 10 minutes, or until the tops are nicely browned.

FISHERMEN'S LANGOUSTE

Insalata d'aligosta Serves 4

This method of serving crawfish dates from the time when the fishermen would be absent for several days from their home port and, having no way to preserve the *langouste* that were caught in their nets, were obliged to cook them themselves.

1 or 2 langoustes *or lobsters (weighing in total about 1 1/2 kilos)*
1 onion (the purple kind are best for this dish)
salt and pepper
2 tbsp wine vinegar
8 tbsp olive oil

Bring seawater or salted water to the boil and cook the *langoustes* for 15 to 20 minutes. Uncover and leave to cool. Chop the onion very finely and mix with half a teaspoon of salt, pepper and vinegar. Beat in the olive oil. Cut the *langouste* in half lengthwise and discard the gills and stomach sac (between the eyes). Remove the coral, if there is any, and the tomally and mix with the sauce. Serve with the *langouste*.

POUTINE FRITTERS

E fritelle di bianchettu Serves 4

Poutine, *alevin* or *bianchettu* are different names for the larvae of sardines. They are about the size of daisy petals and are in season in the winter months. They usually appear after a storm and are fished with very finely meshed nets. I often see men fishing from the pontoons in the port at night, using strong flashlights to attract the *poutine*, a practice which is frowned upon, if not illegal. In fact, the fishing of *poutine*, which was current before the Second World War, may soon be banned. Here are some recipes for the most usual ways of cooking them (while you still can).

180 g plain flour
salt and pepper
1 egg
500 g poutine

Sift the flour and 1 tsp salt into a bowl and make a well in the centre. Stir in the egg and enough cold water to make a batter. Rinse and shake dry the *poutine* and mix with the other ingredients. Drop spoonfuls into fairly hot oil in a deep fryer and cook until golden on both sides. Drain on kitchen paper and serve with lemon wedges.

POUTINE FRITTERS, ANOTHER WAY

E fritelle di bianchettu Serves 4

500 g poutine
2 finely chopped cloves garlic
2 tbsp chopped parsley
100 g plain flour
2 beaten eggs
salt and pepper

Rinse and shake dry the *poutine* and mix with the garlic, parsley, flour, eggs and seasoning. Heat 2 tablespoons of olive oil in a frying-pan and drop spoonfuls of the mixture into it. Fry until golden brown underneath and turn over to fry on the other side. Keep them warm until you have used up all the mixture and serve immediately with lemon wedges.

POUTINE STEW

Bagnapane di bianchettu Serves 4

2 tbsp olive oil
1 onion, finely chopped
2 cloves garlic, crushed and chopped
1 tbsp tomato concentrate
4 potatoes
1 pinch saffron
salt and pepper
500 g poutine
1 tbsp chopped parsley
4 slices country bread, toasted and rubbed with garlic

Heat the oil in a saucepan and gently fry the onion and garlic until soft. Stir in the tomato paste. Peel and thinly slice the potatoes and add to the pan with the saffron. Cook, stirring carefully, for a few minutes and add 750 ml water.

Bring to the boil and season with salt and pepper. Lower heat and simmer for about 10 minutes, or until the potatoes are nearly tender. Add the *poutine* and continue simmering for about 10 minutes. Check the seasoning, sprinkle with parsley and serve over the garlic-rubbed toast.

POUTINE SOUP

Aziminu di bianchettu

Serves 4

1 onion, finely chopped
2 tbsp olive oil
2 cloves garlic, crushed and chopped
3 tomatoes, peeled and chopped
pinch of saffron
salt and pepper
300 g poutine
slices of toasted, slightly stale country-style bread

Cook the onion in the oil until soft. Add the garlic and tomatoes and cook, stirring, for a minute or two. Cover with about 1 litre water, add the saffron and season with salt and pepper. Bring to the boil, then simmer for 20 minutes. Add the *poutine* and cook for a further 5 minutes. Sprinkle with parsley and serve poured over the toasted bread.

SKATE WITH GARLIC

Squale ou agliolu Serves 4

1 kilo skate wings
2 tbsp vinegar
3 large cloves garlic, crushed and chopped
1/2 tsp salt
1 hot red chilli pepper, deseeded or 1/2 tsp chilli purée
1/2 wine glass olive oil

Cut the skate wings into medium-sized pieces. Put them into a large frying-pan and half cover with boiling water. Add the vinegar and bring back to the boil. Cook for about 2 minutes, turning the fish over once. Meanwhile pound together the garlic, salt and chilli pepper to a paste and whisk in the oil. Remove the fish pieces with a slotted spoon and keep them warm by covering with a plate or kitchen foil. Pour away two-thirds of the liquid and add the oil mixture to the liquid remaining in the pan. Boil together for one minute, lower the heat and put back the pieces of fish. Cook for 2 or 3 minutes longer, spooning the sauce over the fish.

MORAY EEL WITH RAISINS

Murena inca uvi seccati Serves 4

A fisherman once told me that if you put a moray eel, a lobster and an octopus in the same fish tank together, there would be a stand-off as they are each capable of killing the other. This fierce fish is highly appreciated and makes for fine eating. In northern countries, the conger eel is more readily available and may, perhaps, be a substitute.

1 tbsp olive oil
4 thick slices moray eel (the body, not the tail)
3 ripe tomatoes, skinned and chopped
2 cloves garlic, crushed and chopped
2 tbsp parsley, chopped
60 g raisins
1 glass dry white wine
1 bay leaf
salt and pepper

Oil the bottom of an ovenproof dish and put in the pieces of fish side by side. Mix the rest of the ingredients, seasoning well, and spread them over the fish. Cover with a piece of aluminium foil and bake in a preheated oven (220°C/gas 7) for 30 minutes.

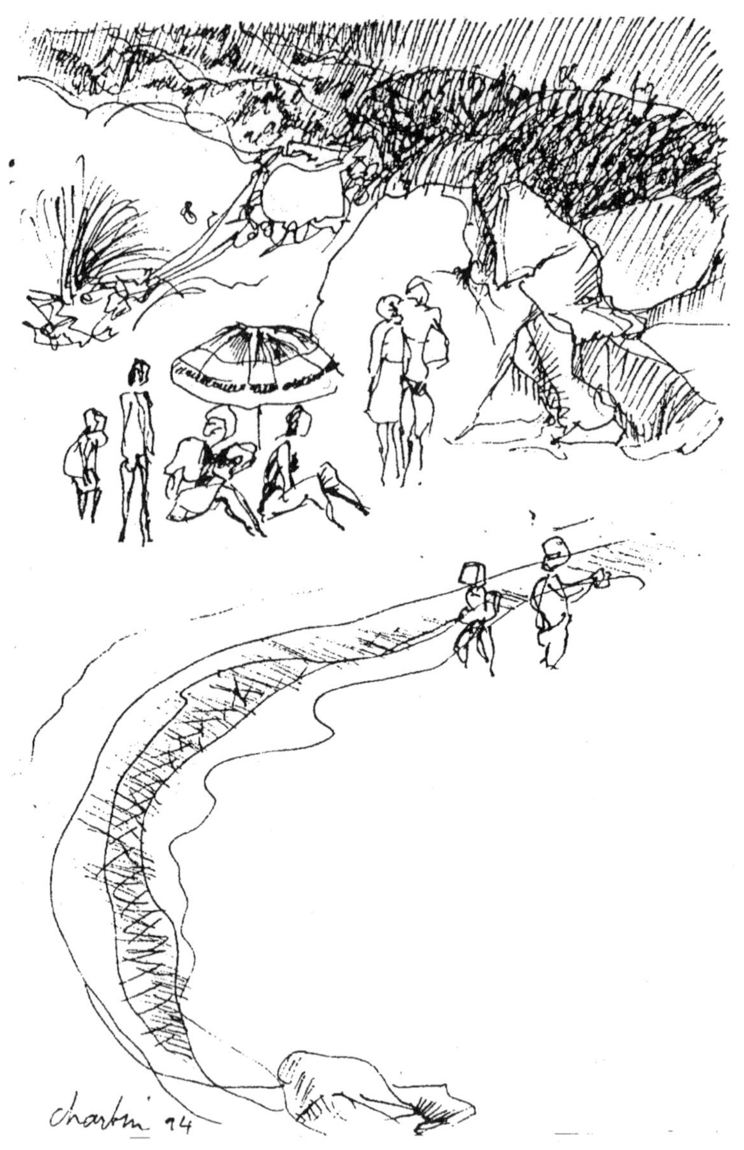

RED MULLET WITH ANCHOVIES

Trigle incu anchiuve Serves 4

Red mullet is one of the most appreciated fish in the Mediterranean and one of the most prolific around the coast of Corsica. They are usually grilled or baked, sometimes wrapped in vine leaves or thin slices of cured ham. The flesh is firm and sweet and the liver has a gamy flavour. The only drawback is that the bones are many and sharp. This recipe comes from Bonifacio, in the south of the island. If you can't find red mullet, you could substitute fresh sardines, such as are often caught in large numbers in British waters. The anchovies that figure in this recipe would, in Corsica, be the salted kind sold from wooden barrels in the markets. They are soaked in cold water for an hour or so before the pink fillets are prised off. Here, anchovies in oil are perfectly acceptable.

8 medium-size red mullet
4 cloves garlic
16 fillets anchovies
½ bunch parsley
3 tomatoes peeled, seeded and chopped, or 2 tbsp tomato concentrate
1 cup fresh breadcrumbs
3 tbsp olive oil
pepper

Scale and clean the fish leaving the livers (a delicacy) inside. Crush and finely chop the garlic, finely chop the anchovies and parsley and mix with the tomatoes or paste. Oil a baking dish just large enough to hold the fish side by side and spread the mixture over the bottom. Lay the fish on top, season with a little pepper and sprinkle with the breadcrumbs. Drizzle with the rest of the oil and cook in a preheated oven (210°C/gas 6/7) for 15 minutes.

GOLDEN FRIED SARDINES

Sardelles dorate e fritte Serves 4

16 medium or 24 small sardines
3 eggs
salt and pepper
flour

Prepare the sardines as in the succeeding recipe. Beat the eggs together and season well with the salt and pepper. Put some flour into a shallow bowl. Heat some oil or lard in a deep frying-pan or fryer. Take a sardine by its tail and dip it first into the egg and then the flour. Lower it into the hot fat. Do the same with the others but don't overcrowd the pan. Fry until golden and drain on kitchen paper. Keep the cooked sardines warm in a low oven. Serve with wedges of lemon.

SARDINES STUFFED WITH CHARD AND BROCCIU

Sardelle incu bietulle Serves 4

Until around 1920, sardines and anchovies formed an important part of the island's economy, with the main part of the catch being exported to Italy or Marseilles. The fish were packed into large wooden or ceramic casks in concentric circles layered with salt to preserve them. Both anchovies and sardines from Corsica have a very high reputation for excellence. Alas, nowadays, the amount of the catch has diminished to about one tonne a year of each, although they are still appreciated and prepared in a variety of ways. Did you know that if you cut the heads off sardines they don't smell when you cook them?

16 large or 24 small sardines
200 g cooked Swiss chard leaves
200 g brocciu
1 large or 2 small eggs
1 large clove garlic, crushed and chopped
2 tbsp parsley, chopped
salt and pepper
fresh breadcrumbs
2 tbsp olive oil

Scale, behead and gut the sardines, opening them down the belly. Remove the backbones. These come away quite easily if you press your thumb down the outside of the back. Rinse and pat dry, then open them out like butterflies. Squeeze the chard well in your hands to remove any moisture and chop finely. Crush the *brocciu* with a fork. Beat the egg and mix with the *brocciu*, chard, garlic and parsley; season well. Lay the sardines skin-side down, with their tails facing away from you. Put some stuffing on each fish and roll it up towards the tail. Put them in one layer in an oiled shallow baking dish and sprinkle with breadcrumbs. Drizzle the oil over and cook in a hot oven (225°C/gas7) for 10 minutes.

You can also make these without the Swiss chard, and they will be called *sardelle incu brocciu*.

SARDINES IN TOMATO SAUCE

Sardelle incu pumate Serves 4

1 onion, chopped
3 tbsp olive oil
2 cloves garlic, crushed and chopped
1 tbsp tomato concentrate
5 tomatoes, peeled and chopped, or 1 tin chopped tomatoes
salt and pepper
16 medium or 24 small sardines
3 tbsp fresh breadcrumbs

Cook the onion in a little olive oil until soft. Add the garlic and tomato concentrate and cook for 1 minute. Add the chopped tomatoes and season with salt and pepper. Bring to the boil, then simmer, covered, for 30 minutes. Meanwhile prepare the fish as before. Rinse and pat dry. Spread half the sauce in the bottom of a shallow ovenproof dish and lay the sardines on top in a single layer. Season with salt and pepper then cover with the rest of the sauce. Sprinkle with the breadcrumbs and drizzle a little more olive oil over the top. Cook in a hot oven (225°C/gas 7) for 15 minutes.

SARDINES WITH FIGS

Sardelle incu ficchi Serves 4

8 large or 12 medium sardines
2 or 3 fresh figs
2 large ripe tomatoes
1 tbsp parsley, chopped
1 or 2 cloves garlic, finely chopped
2 tbsp fresh breadcrumbs
salt and pepper
2 tbsp olive oil

Prepare the sardines as before. Rinse and pat dry. Cut the figs into quarters lengthways. Lay out the sardines skin-side down with the tails facing away from you. Season them with salt and pepper and roll each one around a piece of fig, rolling towards the tail. Put them in a shallow baking dish in one layer with the tails sticking up. The dish should be just large enough to hold them comfortably. Skin and seed the tomatoes and dice the flesh. Put this over and between the sardines. Sprinkle with the parsley, garlic, breadcrumbs and seasoning. Drizzle the olive oil over the top and cook in a preheated oven (220°C/gas 7) for 10 to 15 minutes. Serve hot or cold with wedges of lemon.

SEA BREAM WITH TOMATOES

Urata incu pumatit Serves 4

Sea bream of all kinds are caught in Corsican waters, particularly around Ajaccio. They are all good to eat and are cooked in a variety of ways: baked, poached, grilled and stuffed. Probably the star of all bream is the gilt-head, called *urata* in Corsica.

1 sea bream weighing about 1 ½ kilos
5 tbsp plain flour
5 tbsp olive oil
1 medium onion, chopped
2 cloves garlic crushed and chopped
4 large tomatoes skinned, seeded and chopped
50 g black olives, pitted
salt and pepper

Scale and gut the sea bream and cut it into 4 thick slices. Coat with flour (put the flour into a plastic bag and shake the pieces of fish in it) and fry in 3 tbsp of the oil until golden on both sides. Keep to one side. Clean out the frying-pan and heat the rest of the oil. Fry the onions and garlic gently until soft and add the tomatoes. Season well and simmer for 10 minutes. Put the fish pieces into a baking dish and cover with the sauce. Scatter the olives over the top and cook in a preheated oven (220°C/gas 7) for 10 minutes.

As sea bream is so expensive, you could leave the fish whole, thus saving the head and tail pieces; or you could substitute cod or hake steaks.

BAKED SEA BREAM WITH BROCCIU

Urata incu brocciu Serves 4

1 sea bream weighing about 1 1/2 kilos
60 g soft breadcrumbs
100 ml milk
2 tbsp finely chopped onion
1 tbsp olive oil
1 clove garlic, crushed and chopped
1/2 tsp thyme leaves
200 g brocciu
8 thin rashers panzetta
1/2 litre light stock or white wine
salt and pepper

Scale and clean the fish if this hasn't already been done. Soak the breadcrumbs in the milk. Gently fry the onion in oil until soft and add the garlic and thyme. Cook for another minute and let cool. Squeeze out the breadcrumbs with your hands and mix them with the *brocciu* and the cooked onion and garlic. Season the inside of the fish and stuff with this mixture. Cut four of the slices of *panzetta* into three pieces each. Make slanting cuts in the sides of the fish and insert the pieces of *panzetta*. Lay the fish in an oiled baking dish and cover with the rest of the *panzetta*. Pour in enough stock or wine to come halfway up the fish and cook in a preheated medium oven (210°C/gas 6/7) for 25 to 30 minutes or until the flesh comes away from the backbone when pulled with the tip of a knife.

BAKED SEA BREAM WITH HERBS

Urata incu l'erba Serves 6

2 sea bream, about 1 kilo each
4 sprigs fresh thyme
4 sprigs fresh rosemary or fennel
1 glass dry white wine
100 g black olives
2 bay leaves
1 lemon, thinly sliced
4 cloves garlic, sliced
2 tomatoes, sliced
salt and pepper

Scale and gut the fish, sprinkle the cavities with salt and pepper and put a sprig of thyme and one of rosemary or fennel inside each. Place the fish side by side in an oiled baking dish and pour the wine over them. Arrange the rest of the herbs, the olives and the lemon, garlic and tomato slices over and around them. Season with salt and pepper and drizzle olive oil over the top. Bake in a preheated oven (220°C/Gas 7) for 20 to 25 minutes, or until the flesh just comes away from the backbone when the tip of a knife is inserted.

TROUT IN RED WINE SAUCE

Azimu di Corte Serves 4

Trout are abundant in the rivers and lakes of Corsica. Smaller than the trout we usually see in Britain, they are renowned for their delicacy, although you'll only be able to taste them by making friends with a fisherman or ordering them in one of the mountain restaurants or inns. In either case they may be cooked for you in the traditional way, grilled on a large stone which has been heated white-hot in a wood fire and rubbed with butter.

If you cook them beside the river where they were caught (surely the most satisfying way), you will find a choice of stones in the river for the purpose. Choose two of the flattest and heat them in a wood fire. Rub one with oil or butter and cook one side of the gutted fish for five minutes. Remove the second stone from the fire and cook the fish on the other side. You will need thick gloves for handling the stones.

Legend has it that in the year 1872 the wine production around the town of Corte, in the centre of the island, was so great that there was no more room for wine in the cellars of the town. The surplus was thrown into the local river, the Restonica and, one hour later, the inhabitants of the town were astonished to see hundreds of drunken trout floating belly up. So was born the idea of trout in red wine sauce.

2 shallots, finely chopped
1 red or green pepper, finely chopped
2 cloves garlic, crushed and chopped
1 tbsp tomato concentrate, or 3 ripe tomatoes, peeled and chopped
1 bay leaf, 2 sprigs thyme, 1 sprig rosemary
½ bottle dry red wine
4 trout
seasoned flour, salt and freshly ground pepper

To make the sauce, which bears a strong resemblance to *raito* sauce, popular in Provence and dating back to the Phoenicians, heat 1 tbsp of olive oil in a thick-bottomed saucepan and gently fry the shallots and pepper until soft. Add the garlic and stir in the tomato concentrate (or chopped tomatoes) and herbs. Stir for a minute and pour in the wine. Season lightly and bring to the boil. Turn the heat down to simmer and reduce the sauce by half.

Meanwhile deal with the trout. They will probably have been cleaned but, if not, it is quite easy to do. Slit them down the belly and pull out everything inside. Rinse them under cold water, scraping out any blood along the backbone, and wipe with kitchen paper. Put 2 tbsp flour in a plastic bag with a teaspoon each of salt and pepper. Put the trout in and shake them about so that they are coated with flour. Heat 2 tbsp of olive oil in a large frying-pan and fry the trout over a medium heat for about 4 minutes on each side. They are done when the flesh just comes away from the backbone when you push it with a knife. Serve hot with the sauce spooned over.

You can also cook the trout directly in the sauce, in which case you do not need to flour them. They will take about 10 minutes to cook. Turn them once.

TROUT IN GARLIC SAUCE

Truite in agliolu Serves 4

4 trout
salt and flour for dredging
7 tbsp olive oil
5 cloves garlic, crushed and chopped
½ glass white wine vinegar
1 bay leaf
1 sprig thyme
1 sprig rosemary
salt and pepper

Clean the trout as above, rub with salt and dredge with flour. Shake off the excess flour and fry the fish in 2 tbsp of olive oil for 4 minutes each side. Keep warm in low oven and clean out the frying-pan. Heat the rest of the oil and fry the garlic over a low heat for 1 minute. Add the other ingredients and reduce the sauce by half. Watch out for the vinegar fumes! Serve the trout with the sauce poured over them. You can also make this dish with sardines or red mullet. Traditionally it is eaten cold like an escabeche but I like it just as well hot.

SEA ANEMONE FRITTERS

Fritelle di bilorbi Serves 4

The following is one of those mythical recipes that you read about and wonder if anyone has really tasted. I have done it for you and promise that it is delicious.

For the batter:
200 g plain flour
pinch of salt
1 egg separated, plus 1 egg white
up to one-third of a litre of water

16 sea anemones

Sift the flour and salt into a bowl and make a well in the centre. Separate the egg and add the yolk to the flour. Gradually work in the flour from the sides, adding enough water to make a batter the consistency of cream, and beating to eliminate lumps. Leave the batter to stand for at least 30 minutes.

Meanwhile deal with the sea anemones. Wash to rid them of any sand and cut any large ones in half from top to bottom. Pat dry with kitchen paper.

Whisk the egg whites with a pinch of salt and fold into the batter. Dip the sea anemones into the batter and fry in hot fat until golden, turning once. Drain on kitchen paper and sprinkle with salt. Serve hot with wedges of lemon.

RAGOÛT OF TUNA

Tianu di tonnu Serves 4

1 thick slice of tuna (800 g to 1 kilo)
6 fillets anchovies, halved
juice of 1 lemon
1 onion, chopped
3 ripe tomatoes, skinned and chopped
2 cloves garlic, crushed
1 bay leaf, 1 sprig thyme, 1 sprig rosemary
100 ml dry white wine
3 tbsp olive oil, salt and pepper

With a small, sharp knife make slits in the tuna and insert the halved fillets of anchovy. Put the fish on a plate and pour over the juice of the lemon and 1 tbsp of olive oil. Turn the fish over and marinate for 2 hours, turning from time to time. Drain, saving the marinade. Heat 2 tbsp olive oil in a large fireproof baking dish and brown the fish on both sides. Remove the fish and gently fry the onion in the same oil. Add the tomatoes, garlic, herbs and white wine. Put the tuna, with the reserved marinade, on top, and season with salt and pepper. Do not add too much salt because of the anchovies. Cook in a preheated (220°C/gas 7) oven for 10 minutes. Take the dish out and adjust seasoning if need be. Baste with the sauce, cover with a sheet of aluminium foil and continue cooking for 10 minutes.

CONFIT OF TUNA

Tonnu incu l'oliu

Tuna caught around the Corsican coastline has always had a high reputation for quality although the annual catch nowadays is somewhat less than six tonnes a year. It used to be salted before being exported and sometimes it was preserved in oil as in this recipe. The amount of oil and salt depends on the size of the receptacles. This recipe uses 2 kilos of fish. If you use less, reduce the cooking time.

a slice of tuna weighing 2 kilos
sea salt
4 bay leaves, olive oil to cover

Put the fish in a saucepan and cover with cold water. Add 35 grams of sea salt per litre of water. Bring to the boil and simmer for 30 minutes. Remove with a large fish slice and leave to cool. Remove the skin and bones carefully, separating the fish into large chunks. Put the fish into one or two lidded containers, with the bay leaves, and cover with olive oil. The tuna will keep perfectly in a fridge for up to two weeks.

GAME AND BIRDS

CIVET OF HARE

U tianu di levru Serves 8 to 10

The numbers of wild hare have diminished considerably since the Second World War, no doubt due to the poaching during those lean years, but they can still be found fairly easily in the Cortenais and Balagne regions, in the centre and north-west of the island. This dish is lovely eaten with *pulenda*, a purée made with chestnut flour (see below, page 184).

1 hare
1 bottle dry white wine
1 large onion, chopped
3 cloves garlic, crushed
1 bay leaf, 2 sprigs thyme
4 tbsp olive oil
1 tbsp plain flour
1 tbsp tomato concentrate
4 tbsp brandy
salt and pepper
the blood of the hare if possible (keep this in the deep-freeze until you are ready to cook the dish)

Cut the hare into pieces and, as long as it hasn't been hung too long, marinate in the wine with the onion, garlic and herbs in a china or glass dish for up to 48 hours. Strain the pieces of hare and vegetables and wipe the meat dry. Retain the marinade itself. Heat the oil in a heavy-bottomed fireproof dish and fry the pieces of hare with the strained onions and garlic until they are golden brown. Lower the heat and sprinkle in the flour. Stir until the flour starts to colour and add the tomato concentrate. Flame with the brandy and add the wine. Stir in the crusty bits from the bottom of the pan and add the seasonings and herbs from the marinade. Cover the casserole and cook over a low heat or in a low oven (180°C/gas 4) for about 1 1/2 hours, or until the hare is tender. Beat the blood, if using, then add a ladleful of the hot sauce, beating all the time. Stir this into the casserole and bring back just to boiling-point before serving. Do not let it re-boil or it will curdle.

BLACKBIRDS WITH CHERRIES

I merrulli chjarasgi Serves 4

Until a few years ago Corsicans ate blackbirds and thrushes, which were considered as legitimate game as pheasants, partridges and pigeons. Blackbird pâté was a feature of most restaurant menus and was for sale in any grocery. Although blackbirds are now a protected species they are probably still enjoyed in private homes and small *auberges* in the villages. They are delicious simply cooked on spits of myrtle wood in front of an open fire. The birds feed on myrtle berries and taste like a cross between pheasant and pigeon. For the following recipes you could substitute quail.

8 blackbirds or 4 fat quails
250 g sour cherries
8 slices of panzetta
3 tbsp lard or olive oil
1 glass cherry liqueur
salt and pepper

Pluck and singe the birds (if they haven't already been prepared) and cut off the heads and feet. Gut them and put the livers and hearts back inside. Stone the cherries and put two or three inside each bird with a little oil or lard. Season the birds and wrap each one in a slice of *panzetta*, fastening it with a wooden toothpick. Heat the remaining oil or lard in a heavy-bottomed casserole, put in the birds and cover with a lid. Cook gently for about 15 minutes (20 minutes for quail) turning them over from time to time. Remove the birds from the casserole and keep warm. Turn the heat up and cook the rest of the cherries for one minute. Lower the heat, put the birds and any juices back, and continue cooking for 5 minutes. Just before serving add the cherry liqueur and stir in any crusty bits from the bottom of the pan.

BLACKBIRDS IN POTATO BOATS

Merulli incu pommi Serves 4

8 blackbirds or 4 fat quails
8 medium (blackbirds) or 4 large (quails) potatoes
100 g panzetta
4 cloves garlic, crushed
1 glass red wine
1 bay leaf, 2 sprigs rosemary
½ liqueur glass of eau de vie *or brandy*

Prepare the birds as above. Peel the potatoes and cut off a third horizontally. Hollow them out carefully with a spoon to a thickness of about 1 ½ centimetres. Cook them in boiling salted water for about 5 minutes and leave to cool. Alternatively cook them unpeeled in boiling salted water for about 10 minutes then drain and cool them before peeling and hollowing out.

Heat a little oil or lard in a fire-proof shallow casserole and fry the *panzetta* until it is golden. In the same pan, brown the outsides of the potato cases slightly, holding them in place with a fork. Reserve. Then add the birds and brown them all over. Reserve. Add the herbs, red wine and garlic to the *panzetta* and bring to the boil. Lower the heat and gently insert the potato boats with the birds on top. Flame with brandy and baste well. Cook uncovered in a preheated oven (220°C/gas 7), basting from time to time, for 20 to 30 minutes, until the birds are brown and the potatoes cooked through. Although not crispy, the potatoes will be delicious because all the juices will have collected where you scooped them out.

It is advisable to truss the birds as otherwise their wings stick out and their legs stick up and they look disconcertingly like fat little headless men sitting in chairs.

CHICKEN WITH SAGE

U pudestru incu a salvia Serves 4 to 6

Sage grows wild in Corsica and is often used in cooking. The following recipe includes a stuffing which is reminiscent of English sage and onion. In Mediterranean countries poultry is more often braised in a casserole than baked in the oven in an open dish. If you buy a chicken in a butcher's shop do not be surprised if it is weighed with its feet, head and innards, and take that into account when reckoning up the price. Don't worry, the butcher will prepare it for you.

120 ml milk
3 cloves garlic, crushed and chopped
250 g stale breadcrumbs
8 sage leaves, chopped
1 oven-ready chicken of 1 1/2 to 2 kilos
3 tbsp olive oil
salt and pepper
1 glass white wine or water

Put the garlic and milk in a small saucepan and bring to the boil. Simmer for 3 minutes and pour over the breadcrumbs. Leave to cool. Squeeze out the bread, add the sage, salt and pepper and mix well. Stuff the cavity of the chicken with this mixture and truss with thin string or skewers. Heat the olive oil in a big casserole, deep enough to hold the chicken with a lid on, and brown the bird on all sides. Pour the wine or water into the bottom of the casserole and season well. Cover and cook either in a preheated oven (200°C/gas 6) or on top of the stove, for 35 minutes. Turn the chicken over and continue cooking for 35 minutes. Test by inserting the point of a knife or skewer into the inside of the thigh. If the juices run clear the bird is cooked; if not cook for up to 30 minutes more (if the chicken weighs 2 kilos). Cut into pieces and serve with the stuffing, pan juices and fresh vegetables.

CHICKEN WITH TOMATOES AND PEPPERS

U puddastra incu pummate Serves 4 to 6

1 oven-ready chicken of 1 ½ to 2 kilos
2 tbsp olive oil
2 red or green peppers
2 cloves garlic crushed
½ glass wine (red, white or rosé)
500 g ripe tomatoes, peeled and chopped
1 hot red chilli pepper or ½ tsp cayenne
1 bay leaf, 2 sprigs thyme, 8 chopped leaves basil
salt and pepper

Cut the chicken into serving pieces and brown in the olive oil in a casserole or saucepan. Deseed and cut the peppers into thin strips and add, with the garlic, to the casserole and cook until soft. Pour in the wine, boil for 1 minute and add the other ingredients. Stir, cover and cook over a low heat for one hour. Serve with pasta.

PIGEONS WITH PEAS

I pincuoni incu i pisi Serves 4

Pigeons are as expensive as pheasants in France and are often imported from England.

2 tbsp olive oil
1 slice of bread cut into triangles
100 g panzetta
2 plump pigeons
2 onions
1 tbsp tomato concentrate
1 bay leaf, 2 sprigs thyme
800 g podded peas
1 tbsp butter, salt and pepper

Heat the oil in a heavy-bottomed casserole and fry the bread on both sides. Reserve. Cut the *panzetta* into cubes and lightly brown in the oil. Remove with a slotted spoon and reserve. Remove the livers of the pigeons and hold in reserve. Cut the birds in half lengthways and cook in the oil until browned on all sides. Remove and reserve. Chop the onions finely and cook in the oil until soft. Stir in the tomato and add the pigeons, *panzetta* and herbs and just enough hot water to cover the birds. Season and bring to the boil before lowering heat and simmering, covered, for 20 minutes. Add the peas and continue cooking until the pigeons are tender, about 20 minutes. Meanwhile cook the livers in the butter, season and mash onto the croûtons. Serve them with the pigeons.

ROAST WOODCOCK

I bicazzi arustiti

Serves 4

2 tbsp olive oil or lard
5 woodcock
500 ml red wine
2 bay leaves
1/2 glass water
salt and pepper
1 liqueur glass cognac
4 small slices bread

Heat the oil or lard in a fireproof dish just large enough to hold the birds together side by side. Brown the birds all over and add the wine, bay leaves, water and seasonings. Cook them in a hot oven (225°C/gas 7/8) for 10 to 15 minutes. Take the birds out of the dish, cut them in half lengthways and discard the entrails, keeping the livers to one side. Keep four of the birds warm and remove the flesh of the fifth. Chop the flesh up with the livers and mix in the brandy. Season well. Meanwhile reduce the sauce left in the oven dish to half the quantity and toast the bread. Spread the liver mixture on to the toasts and put 2 halves of the woodcocks on each piece. Pour some of the sauce around the toast and serve hot.

PARTRIDGE WITH CABBAGE

Parmici incu u carbuscui Serves 4

This recipe is very similar to the classic French dish of the same name, but with the addition of tomato and a hot red pepper.

2 partridges
1 medium sized cabbage
5 crushed cloves garlic
1 bouquet garni (parsley, thyme, bay leaf)
1 tbsp tomato concentrate
1 hot red chilli pepper
3 tbsp olive oil
salt

Cut the partridges into quarters and brown the pieces on all sides in the olive oil. Add the tomato concentrate, bouquet garni, red chilli pepper and garlic and cook together for 2 minutes. Add a glass of water, season with salt and cook, covered, over a low heat, for about 20 minutes. Meanwhile core then cut the cabbage into eight pieces from top to bottom. Blanch for a minute or two in boiling salted water. Drain and add to the partridges. Cook, covered, for 20 minutes. Remove the bouquet garni and red chilli pepper before serving.

RABBIT WITH GARLIC AND WINE

Sunigliulu incu l'agliu e vinu

There are a lot of rabbits in Corsica, particularly in the Balagne region, in the north-west, where they constitute a problem for farmers. This is a very simple recipe that would also work well with chicken.

1 rabbit, skinned and gutted
4 shallots
4 to 6 cloves garlic
1 hot red chilli pepper
2 bay leaves, 2 sprigs thyme, 1 sprig rosemary
3 glasses red or white wine
2 tbsp olive oil or lard
salt and pepper

Cut the rabbit into serving pieces, peel and slice the shallots and crush and chop the garlic. Heat the oil or lard in a fireproof casserole and brown the rabbit. Add the shallots and cook until soft. Add the garlic, whole chilli and herbs, cook for a minute or two and add the wine. Season and bring to the boil. Lower the heat and simmer, covered, for one hour, turning the rabbit pieces over from time to time. Remove the bay leaves and chilli before serving with polenta or potatoes.

LAMB AND GOAT

After pigs, sheep and goats provide the largest source of meat in the traditional diet. Corsican sheep are small, weighing about 35 kilos, and are well adapted to the mountainous terrain of the island. They account for some 83 per cent of the *troupes* or flocks, with about 3 per cent made up of the Sardinian breed and the rest a cross between the two. They are raised in the tradition of transhumance, spending the summer months in the high plains and the winters in the valleys where they feed on the many herbs that make up the *maquis*, the fragrant undergrowth that covers much of the island. They are mainly bred for their milk though older animals may be slaughtered for their meat and in the spring the surplus male lambs are also killed, usually for consumption at the Easter festivities. The meat is of a high standard and has its own label of authenticity.

The goats of the island have an even higher reputation for quality and are the preferred meat for feast days, although they too are principally bred for their milk. The race is very ancient and seems close to the breeds that live wild in central Asia. The young male goats or kids are slaughtered in time for the end-of-year festivities. The meat is either cooked with wine and herbs or roasted in the oven.

MILK-FED LAMB

U tianu d'agnellu Serves 4 to 6

2 kilos milk-fed lamb (boned leg, loin or shoulder)
2 tbsp olive oil
1 onion, finely chopped
3 cloves garlic, crushed
1 tbsp tomato purée
2 tomatoes, chopped
3 glasses wine (red, white or rosé)
1 bay leaf, 2 sprigs thyme,2 sprigs rosemary
salt and pepper

Cube the lamb and brown in batches in the oil in a large frying-pan. Put it into a saucepan or casserole as it is cooked. Lower the heat and gently fry the onion until it is soft. Add the garlic and stir in the tomato purée. Add the fresh tomatoes and pour in the wine. Cook for a minute while you stir in any crusty bits. Pour over the lamb in the casserole and add the herbs. Season to taste, bring the wine to the boil and then lower the heat. Cover tightly and simmer for 1 to 1 ½ hours. Serve with *pulenda* (see page 184) or polenta.

LAMB STEW WITH HARICOTS

Tianu di agnelli incu fasgioli Serves 6

1 ½ kilos shoulder of lamb
300 g large white dried beans soaked overnight
2 tbsp lard or olive oil
150 g panzetta, *cubed*
1 large onion, chopped
4 cloves garlic, crushed and chopped
3 tbsp tomato concentrate
1 bay leaf, 2 sprigs thyme, 1 sprig rosemary
salt and pepper

Cut the meat into large cubes and remove any excess fat. Drain the beans, re-cover with fresh salted water and cook for one hour. Drain. Meanwhile, heat the oil in a casserole and brown the meat and *panzetta* on all sides. Add the onion and cook until soft. Stir in the garlic, tomato and herbs, add the beans and seasonings and enough water to cover. Bring to the boil, lower heat and simmer, covered, for one hour or until beans are soft and the meat is tender. Add hot water if necessary during cooking. The finished dish should be quite juicy. If you haven't time to soak the beans overnight, bring them to the boil, turn off the heat and leave them for half an hour, then strain them and cook as above

KID STEW

U tianu di cabri Serves 4

The following method of cooking *cabri* (young goat or kid) is used all over the island. It is a dish served on feast days, usually with *pulenda*. Most people have strong views on whether it should be made with red, white or rosé wine. The flesh of the *cabri* is thought superior to that of lamb.

2 tbsp lard or olive oil
2 kilos cabri, *taken off the bone and cut into large cubes*
1 tbsp tomato concentrate
4 cloves garlic, crushed
1 bay leaf, 2 sprigs thyme,2 sprigs rosemary
½ bottle red or dry white wine
salt and pepper

Heat the oil or lard in a heavy-bottomed casserole and brown the pieces of kid on all sides. Remove them with a slotted spoon and set aside. Stir in the tomato, garlic and herbs and cook for one minute. Add the wine and bring to the boil. Reduce by half. Put the meat back and season the sauce. Stir to coat the pieces of meat, reduce the heat and cook, covered, for one hour. Serve with polenta or *pulenda* (see page 184).

SWEET AND SOUR LAMB STEW

Agnello a l'agru dolce — Serves 4 to 6

The following is a very old recipe. It is important to use good quality wine vinegar.

1 ½ kilos of lamb on the bone (shoulder or leg) or 1 kilo off the bone
2 onions, chopped
3 cloves garlic, crushed
3 tbsp olive oil or lard
2 sprigs each rosemary and thyme
1 glass wine vinegar
1 tbsp sugar
150 g slightly stale bread
2 tbsp chopped parsley
salt and pepper

Cut the meat into large cubes and remove excess fat. Heat the oil or lard in a saucepan and fry the meat until brown all over. Remove the meat, lower heat and cook the onions until soft. Put the meat and any juices back in the pan and add the garlic, herbs and salt and pepper. Cook, covered, for one hour or until the meat is very tender. Dissolve the sugar in the vinegar. Cut the bread into small cubes and soak in the vinegar for a minute or two. Squeeze out between your hands and sprinkle over the meat together with the parsley. Stir and cook together for a minute or two and serve hot. You could replace the lamb with young goat or kid (*cabri*).

LAMB WITH OLIVES

Agnellu incu i alvi Serves 6

1 ½ kilos lamb cut in cubes (boned shoulder or leg)
2 tbsp olive oil
200 g panzetta, *cubed*
2 medium onions, peeled and chopped
2 tbsp tomato concentrate
1 tbsp plain flour
3 cloves garlic, crushed
1 bay leaf, 2 sprigs rosemary, 4 sprigs thyme
½ bottle red or rosé wine
salt and pepper
4 carrots, peeled and sliced
150 g green olives

Remove excess fat from the lamb. Heat the oil in a large casserole and fry the meat in batches until brown on all sides. Remove with a slotted spoon and reserve. Fry the *panzetta* until golden. Lower heat and cook the onions until they are soft. Stir in the tomato and flour and cook for a minute or two. Put back the lamb and any juices and add the garlic and herbs. Raise heat and pour in the wine, stirring in any crusty bits from the bottom of the casserole. When the wine comes to the boil add just enough hot water to cover meat and season well. Lower the heat to simmer and cook, covered, for 1 hour. Add the carrots and rinsed olives and continue cooking for 30 minutes. Skim off excess fat from the top of the meat and serve with pasta or potatoes.

This stew is even better eaten the day after you have made it; the flavours have had time to blend and it is also easier to take the cold fat off the top.

STUFFED SHOULDER OF KID OR LAMB

Spalla da caprettu pienna Serves 4 to 6

500 g raw spinach or Swiss chard
*1 shoulder of lamb or kid (*cabri*)*
200 g minced pork
200 g minced veal
1 tbsp chopped parsley
1 egg, beaten
3 tbsp olive oil
2 sprigs rosemary
1 glass red wine

Cook the spinach or chard (the green leaves only, not the stalks) in a little salted water for 5 minutes, drain well and chop finely. Bone (or ask the butcher to bone) the shoulder of lamb or kid and lay it out flat on a board, skin side down. Keep the bones. Mix the pork and veal with the cooked and chopped greens, the parsley and the egg and season well. Spread the filling down the middle of the shoulder, roll up and tie at intervals with string, making sure the filling can't fall out. Rub the meat with oil and season with salt and pepper. Put in a baking dish with the bones and place the rosemary on top of the meat. Roast the meat for 20 minutes to the pound (with stuffing) in a fairly hot (220°C/gas 7) oven. Test for doneness by sticking a skewer into the thickest part of the meat. If the juices run clear the meat is cooked through. Keep the meat warm and put the pan over a low heat. Pour off any excess fat, scrape up any crusty bits from the bottom of the pan and add one glass of red wine. Let the sauce bubble together for a few minutes and check seasoning. Remove the bones and strain into sauce boat. Keep warm. Remove the string from the meat and cut into thickish slices. Serve with the sauce on the side.

ROAST SHOULDER OR LEG OF LAMB

Spalla o cusciottu d'agnellu Serves 3 to 4

Often a whole kid or *cabri* is cooked on a spit in front of the fire, particularly to celebrate Christmas. At Easter it would be a young lamb. The meat is basted with a mixture of oil and wine vinegar, garlic and salt and pepper. Here is a recipe for a shoulder or leg of milk-fed lamb.

1 shoulder or leg of milk-fed lamb on the bone
2 cloves garlic
3 branches parsley
3 tbsp olive oil
1 tbsp wine vinegar
Salt and pepper

Cut one of the cloves of garlic into slivers and, with a sharp knife, make slits in the meat. Insert slivers of garlic and sprigs of parsley into the slits. Rub the joint with a third of your oil and sprinkle with salt and pepper. Finely chop the second clove of garlic and mix with the vinegar and rest of the oil and salt and pepper in a small bowl. If you have a spit, cook the lamb on it for about 30 minutes, basting with the garlic and oil mix from time to time. The skin should be crisp and golden. If you do not have a grill, put the meat in a baking tray and cook in the oven (220°C/gas 7) in the same way, also basting from time to time. If you prefer your meat well done, cook the lamb for 15 minutes longer. The same method is used for cooking young goat or kid. The times given here are for very small joints of the youngest lamb. If you are trying this with more orthodox British meat, time it as you would your usual roast.

KID OR LAMB STEW WITH NEW POTATOES

Tianu di caprettu i pommi novi Serves 6

1 1/2 kilos boned shoulder of lamb or kid
3 tbsp olive oil
2 medium onions, chopped
2 cloves garlic, crushed
3 tbsp tomato concentrate
2 tbsp plain flour
salt and pepper
1 bay leaf, 2 sprigs thyme
1 kilo new potatoes

Cut the meat into pieces and remove excess fat. Heat the oil in a large saucepan or casserole and brown the meat all over. Add the onions half-way through and cook until soft. Add the garlic and tomato concentrate and stir for a minute. Sprinkle with the flour and cook, stirring, until the flour begins to colour. Cover with cold water and bring to the boil. Lower the heat and skim off any scum that comes to the surface. Repeat until the top of the stew is clear. Season with salt and pepper and add the herbs. Cook, covered, for 45 minutes. Scrub the potatoes and add to the pan; continue cooking for 45 minutes. Serve very hot.

LAMB OR KID'S TRIPE

I tripette Serves 6

Tripe is very popular in Corsica and has nothing in common with the disgusting, slimy stuff cooked with milk and onions that used to be served in English hotel dining-rooms. Here it is cooked in a zingy wine and tomato sauce.

1 1/2 kilos tripe
3 tbsp olive oil
1 large onion, finely sliced
100 g panzetta, *chopped*
4 cloves garlic, crushed and chopped
2 tbsp tomato concentrate
1 hot red chilli pepper
1 bay leaf, 1 sprig thyme, 1 sprig rosemary
2 glasses white wine
salt and pepper

Wash the tripe thoroughly in running water. This is very important. Cut into strips and cook in boiling salted water for 15 minutes. Strain and keep aside. Heat the oil in a heavy-bottomed casserole and gently fry the onion and *panzetta* until the onion starts to soften. Add the garlic, tomato concentrate, red chilli pepper and herbs and cook, stirring, for 2 or 3 minutes. Put in the tripe and wine and enough cold water to cover. Season well with salt and plenty of pepper and bring to the boil. Lower heat and cook gently either in the oven (190°C/gas 5), or on top of the stove for about 4 hours, until tender. Stir from time to time to prevent sticking. Remove the chilli and the herbs before serving very hot with boiled or steamed potatoes.

You can also cook this dish with prepared veal or cow's tripe. This is usually sold pre-cooked and will not take as long. Allow about one hour. You can add a calf's or pig's foot, which will make the dish more gelatinous.

RIVIA

Rivia is the name given to brochettes made from the pluck or insides of a young lamb or kid. They are usually cooked over a wood fire while the rest of the animal is slowly roasted. The dish originates in the south of the island in the Sartenais and Porto-Vecchio regions.

heart, liver and spleen of the animal, plus some intestines and crépine *(caul fat)*
3 cloves garlic
2 tbsp vinegar
salt and pepper
3 tbsp water
brochette sticks

Wash the intestines thoroughly under running water. Cut the heart, liver and spleen into equal-sized pieces and thread them on to the brochette sticks. Start cooking over the fire and, when they are nearly done, remove them. Wrap the caul fat around them and interlace the intestine around that, crossing it over like a plait. Crush and chop the garlic and mix it with the vinegar, salt, pepper and water. Roll the brochettes in this mixture (or brush it over) and start cooking them again, this time a little further away from the heat so that they don't burn. Repeat this procedure until the brochettes are golden-brown and crisp.

MISGISCIA

Misgiscia is the name given to meat, usually goat or mutton, which has been marinated and dried in the sun. It is a very old method of preserving meat, used by the Serbians, Albanians and Tibetans among others, and used for all sorts of meat. The meat is cut into strips and put to macerate for 24 hours in vinegar. Then it is drained, dried on a cloth and rubbed with a mixture of garlic, rosemary and salt and pepper. Finally it is threaded on to slips of wood and dried in the sun. Afterwards it can be eaten raw, or it may be cooked over a wood fire with any juices being mopped up on garlic bread. Alternatively, it is sometimes stewed with wine. It seems that the practice of making *misgiscia* has died out in recent years but, with the resurgence of interest in Corsica's culinary heritage, I hope that it will be revived.

THE WHOLE HOG

Traditionally the killing of pigs, known as the *tumbera*, starts on December 13, the festival of Sainte-Lucie. Usually several members of the family or neighbours will join in the preparation of the pâtés, *boudins* (black puddings) and various cured hams and sausages as, for hygienic reasons, the quicker the work is carried out the better. The loin and fillet of the pig will be cured and made into *lonza* and *coppa* and the legs into *prizutta* or ham. The fattier pieces like the breast and neck, will be made into *panzetta* and *vuletta*. The latter is one of the few charcuterie products of Corsica that doesn't have an equivalent in Italy. It is actually the neck and cheek of pork that is cured in salt and dried for about 6 weeks. Another product exclusively Corsican is *figatellu*, an absolutely delicious liver sausage which is also the best known of all Corsican cured meats. It is a U-shaped sausage composed of liver, fat and meat with herbs and wine sometimes added. The proportions of liver to meat vary from village to village, indeed from pig owner to pig owner. In the valley of Prunelli they make a sausage exclusively of liver called *fittonu*.

The *figatellu* is sometimes smoked before being air-dried. After ten days to two weeks it is ready to be cooked and after two to three months it can be eaten raw. When eaten thus it is cut into thick slices; when it is cooked, it is cut into three or four pieces, which are either cooked on a mesh grill or are threaded on to especially long pronged forks to be held over an open wood fire. Any fat that falls is caught on thick slices of country-style bread, to be eaten with the sausage. It can also be served with *pulenda* (the Corsican version of polenta, made with chestnut flour rather than maize) and fried eggs. Another way of dealing with it is to cook it in a tomato sauce with large white beans or with rice. Or you can follow the suggestion of the following recipe.

LENTILS WITH FIGATELLU

Lenticci incu i figatellu Serves 4

Lentils have been cultivated in the Mediterranean since prehistoric times. In Corsica they were mainly grown in the north of the island. This recipe comes from Castagniccia, the area of chestnut forests in the north-east. You could replace the *figatellu* with good meaty sausages, for example the French-style or Toulouse sausages now sold by many butchers.

500 g Puy lentils
250 g figatellu
2 tbsp olive oil
3 cloves garlic, crushed
1 bay leaf, 2 sprigs thyme
salt and pepper

Put the lentils into a saucepan, cover with cold salted water and bring to the boil. Simmer for 5 minutes and drain. Cut the *figatellu* into short lengths and start to fry in a saucepan with the olive oil. When the pieces are nicely browned, add the garlic and herbs and fry together for one minute. Add the lentils and cover with water. Season lightly as the *figatellu* is usually well seasoned. If you are using British-made sausages, use your own judgement, but remember it is easier to add seasoning than to remove it. Cook over a low heat for 30 minutes, adding a little water if the lentils seem to be drying out.

PIG'S STOMACH STUFFED WITH CHARD

A ventra/trippa pienna

700 g Swiss chard
1 small green cabbage
3 medium onions
1 pig's stomach
3 litres pig's blood
600 gms flair fat
2 tbsp chopped parsley
salt and pepper

Wash and shred the Swiss chard (the green leaves only) and the cabbage. Finely chop the onions. Wash the stomach thoroughly under running water and drain it. Strain the blood through a fine sieve and mix it with an equal amount of water. Cut the flair fat into small dice and mix with the vegetables and parsley into the blood. Season well. Stuff the stomach with this mixture and sew up with a butcher's needle and thread. Put into cold salted water and cook over a very low heat for 2 hours. After 2 hours prick the stomach with a needle in several places and increase the heat. Simmer for another 4 hours. This dish is traditionally eaten at Christmas.

BLACK PUDDING WITH ONIONS

Sangui incu civolle

The blood of the pig is also used to make *boudin* or *sangui*, a lighter version of our own black pudding.

some lengths of pig's intestines
2 tbsp lard
1 $^1/_2$ kilos onions, finely chopped
2 $^1/_2$ litres pig's blood
1 litre full-cream milk or light cream
salt and pepper

Wash the intestines extremely well inside and out with a scrubbing brush under running water. Heat the lard and fry the onions until they are soft. Beat the blood so that it does not curdle and stir in the cream or milk. Add the onions and season well with salt and pepper. Knot the intestines at one end and, using a funnel, fill the skins carefully, coiling them as they fall. Do not fill them too full or they will burst on cooking. Knot the other end. The *boudins* must not come in contact with the pan while cooking so it's best to cook them in a wire basket or the sort of vegetable steamer that has little legs at the bottom. Bring some salted water almost to the boil and then remove it from the heat. Lower the *boudins* in their basket into the water and simmer very gently (the water barely moving) for about 20 minutes. Remove them, still in their basket, and leave to get cold. They will keep in a cold place for a couple of days. When you want to eat them, fry, grill or poach them, always over a low heat. They are usually eaten with sauté potatoes but are also delicious served with creamy mash and fried apple slices.

Sometimes apples or raisins are added to the filling and, in the regions that produce citrus fruits, I have heard that they add a sort of mandarin orange marmalade.

STUFFED PIG'S STOMACH
Ghialaticciu

Although you may think it unlikely that you will ever have a pig's stomach to stuff, let alone a pig's heart and tongue with which to stuff it, you never know. You may be invited to a *tumbera* one day so, just in case, here's the recipe.

800 g fatty pork
400 g pig's liver
1 pig's heart
1 pig's tongue
3 cloves garlic
1 glass red wine (the rest of the bottle to be drunk while you're preparing the dish I imagine)
salt and pepper
1 tsp cayenne pepper
1 pig's stomach

Finely chop, or put through a mincer, the pork meat, liver, heart and tongue. Chop the garlic and add to the meat with the red wine and seasonings. Mix with your hands and fry a teaspoonful to check the seasoning. It must be highly seasoned. Wash the stomach very well under running water and drain it. Stuff it carefully with the meats and, using a butcher's needle and thread, sew up the openings. Put into cold salted water and bring slowly to the boil. Before the water comes to the boil, prick the stomach in several places with the needle. Adjust the heat so the water just simmers and cook the stomach for 2 hours or until the skin is cooked. Remove and let it cool completely. The *ghialaticciu* is served cut into slices and is eaten cold, sometimes with a piquant sauce.

If you find yourself with a stomach on your hands but no heart, liver or tongue, do not despair. You can always make *a ventra*, providing of course, that you have some of the pig's blood.

STUFFED APPENDIX

Ventra cortense

My friend Cathy, who makes and sells excellent charcuterie, says the recipe for pig's stomach that I have just recorded is rubbish, which just goes to show that there are different recipes from different parts of the island and each person vilifies the other's. Cathy's comes from Corte, a town in the mountains in the centre. First of all, she says, pig's stomach is altogether too big and too tough and she always uses the appendix as the casing. This makes a sort of large black pudding or *boudin*.

6 medium onions
2 kilos Swiss chard
1 handful oregano
1 handful mint (in Corsica use half quantity of nepita *or calamint)*
2 tbsp lard
about 2 ½ litres pig's blood
1 litre full cream milk or light cream
1 appendix (also known as une poche *or* un sac*)*
salt and pepper

Chop the onions very finely. Wash and chop the green leaves of the chard. Chop the herbs finely. Melt the lard in a large pan and fry the onions very gently until they soften. Add the herbs and chard and cook, stirring, until the vegetables are soft. Leave to cool. Beat the blood and gradually stir in the cream. Strain into a clean bowl, add the herbs and vegetables and season very well. Fill the *poche* with this mixture and sew up carefully. It is important that the *poche* doesn't touch the saucepan when it cooks or it will split. Here is Cathy's method of dealing with the problem. Almost fill a large saucepan with cold salted water. Find a wooden spoon or piece of wood long enough to sit across the saucepan. Tie a piece of string around each end of the *poche* and loop these pieces of string around the wooden spoon. Rest the piece of wood or spoon across the saucepan so that the *poche* is suspended in the water. Cook very slowly for 2 hours then prick the *poche* with a needle in several places. Raise the heat slightly and continue cooking for 3 to 4 hours. The *ventra* can be served hot, sliced, or left to get cold before being sliced and either fried or grilled.

In other parts of the island raisins might be added or the *nepita* replaced with parsley.

RAZZICA

This is a red chilli pepper powder which was used to rub on the outside of cured hams.

1 kilo hot red chilli peppers
250 g plain flour
1 tbsp salt

Cook the chillis in a very low oven (115°C/gas 1/2) for several hours, until they are perfectly dry. Mix enough water with the flour and salt to make a pliable pastry. Crush the chillis into powder and mix with the pastry. Shape into flattish oblongs or squares and cook in a low oven until they are hard. Crush into powder. The pastry is traditionally cooked on chestnut leaves.

BRAWN

U casgiu di porcu

Having dealt with the innards, we may as well go the whole hog and deal with the head and feet of the animal. This is a recipe for brawn, or *fromage de tête* as it is called in French.

1 pig's head
2 pig's trotters
1 onion, quartered
1 bay leaf
2 cloves garlic, crushed
1 glass red wine
1 cup chopped parsley
salt and pepper

Wash the head and trotters thoroughly. Remove the brain and save for another dish. Chop the head into big pieces and put in a large saucepan with the trotters, onion, garlic and bay leaf. Cover the meat with cold, salted water and bring to the boil. Reduce heat to simmer and skim off any scum that comes to the surface. Continue cooking over a very low heat for 4 to 5 hours until the meat falls off the bone. Strain into another saucepan, saving the liquid. Reduce the liquid over a high heat until you have about half a litre. Keep the trotters to eat on another occasion and remove the meat from the head. Cut into small pieces. When the liquid has reduced enough, add the meat and red wine and season to taste. It should be highly seasoned. Cook gently for about 20 minutes and add the parsley. Check the seasoning again and pour into one or several clean bowls. Put it in the fridge to set.

PIG'S LIVER PÂTÉ

Pasitizzu di fecatu di maiale

Sometimes the liver of the pig is made into pâté. The recipe is very simple, relying for flavour on the quality of the pork.

1 large piece of caul or strips of bard or hard fat, to line the terrine
500 g pig's liver
500 g fat belly of pork
1 clove garlic
1 bay leaf, 2 sprigs thyme
2 eggs
1 tbsp plain flour
salt and pepper

If you are using caul fat, soak it in lukewarm water for 30 minutes. Mince the liver and belly of pork twice over. Finely chop the garlic and mash with a little salt. Strip the thyme leaves. Beat the eggs together with the flour and mix with the meat, thyme leaves, garlic and seasoning. Fry a spoonful of the meat to check the seasoning. Line the terrine with the caul or back fat overlapping at the sides. Pile the meat in pushing well into the terrine, and top with the bay leaf. Pull the caul over the top to cover. Put the terrine into a baking dish and pour in enough water to come half way up the side of the dish. If your terrine doesn't have a lid, cover it closely with tinfoil. Cook in a medium oven (185°C/gas 4) for 2 hours. Test it as you would a cake by sticking a skewer into the centre. If it comes out clean, the pâté is cooked.

In Corsica the pâté is often cooked in a sort of wide-necked Kilner jar, in which case it is sterilized for 2 ½ hours. Sometimes the eggs are replaced by a glass of red wine.

WILD BOAR STEW

Tianu di cinghiale Serves 6

Wild boar has been hunted in Corsica since time immemorial and *la chasse* is as prevalent today as it was hundreds of years ago. There are about 30,000 wild boar on the island and each year around 12,000 are hunted and killed. Most of the villages have their own hunts and groups of hunters also exist in the towns. The season starts on August 15 and continues until the first week in January. The hunt usually takes place on Sundays and Wednesdays because there is no school on those days and sons and nephews from the age of about twelve can be initiated into the traditions. Women are almost never invited to take part. Men and boys, often camouflaged as trees, set off with dogs and guns at dawn and come back in the late afternoon to share out their spoils with the village. This is one of the many recipes for cooking the meat.

1 1/2 kilos wild boar off the bone
4 tbsp olive oil
1 onion, chopped
2 shallots, chopped
3 cloves garlic, crushed
3 tbsp tomato concentrate
1 tbsp plain flour
2 tbsp eau de vie *or brandy*
salt and pepper
100 g dried porcini *(optional)*
For the marinade:
1 bottle strong red wine
1 onion, chopped
1 clove garlic, crushed
2 bay leaves, 2 sprigs thyme or nepita, 1 sprig rosemary, 1/2 stick celery, all tied together
2 cloves
10 black peppercorns

Cut the meat into large cubes and put into a bowl with the marinade ingredients for 24 to 48 hours. Strain and dry the meat on paper towels, keeping back the marinade wine and herbs. Heat the oil over a high heat in a large frying-pan and cook the pieces of meat until brown all over. Transfer them to an ovenproof casserole. Lower the heat and fry the onion, shallots, then the garlic, until they are soft. Stir in the tomato concentrate and flour and then pour in the marinade with the bouquet of herbs. Bring to the boil, scraping in any crusty bits at the bottom of the frying-pan. Flame the meat with the *eau de vie* and pour the sauce into the casserole. Season with salt and pepper. Cover with a lid and cook in a moderate oven (400°C/gas 6) or on top of the stove over a very low heat, for 1 ½ hours. Meanwhile, soak the dried mushrooms in warm water for 30 minutes, strain and add to the stew for the last hour of cooking. Serve with *pulenda* (see page 184) if possible, if not, potatoes, large pasta or polenta will do almost as well.

If you cannot find wild boar you can make a passable imitation with pork. Bring the marinade ingredients to the boil and then let the mixture cool before adding 1 ½ kilos of slightly fatty pork. Marinate for at least 48 hours before cooking.

BEEF AND VEAL

Driving the narrow, twisting roads of Corsica can be an exciting experience, especially when you encounter a flock of sheep or goats or a coachload of tourists going the other way – or maybe a family of snuffling pigs, even the odd wild boar. But for me, the strangest sight is a herd of the local breed of nimble small cows that scrambles up the nearest bank out of harm's way. These are allowed to roam during the day, to eat whatever interesting herbs they may find. Calves in Corsica graze the herbs in the meadows until they are 10 to 14 months old and the resulting veal or *manzu* is full of flavour. Here are three popular recipes.

VEAL STEW WITH PEPPERS

Vitellu incu pivaroni Serves 4

1 kilo veal, leg or shoulder, off the bone
2 tbsp olive oil
2 onions, chopped
2 green peppers, seeded and sliced
2 cloves garlic, crushed
2 tomatoes, peeled and chopped
2 glasses dry white or rosé wine
1 bay leaf, 1 sprig thyme, 1 sprig rosemary
salt and pepper

Cut the veal into largish cubes. Heat the oil in a heavy-bottomed casserole and fry the meat on all sides to seal in the juices. Remove with a slotted spoon and reserve. Lower the heat and fry the onions and pepper strips until they soften. Put back the meat with any juices and add the garlic, tomatoes, herbs and wine. Season with salt and pepper. Bring back to the boil and then turn down the heat and simmer, covered, for 1 1/2 hours. Check from time to time that the stew isn't drying out and add a little hot water if need be. Remove the herbs and serve with rice, pasta or new potatoes.

VEAL STEW WITH OLIVES

Tianu di vitellu incu alvia Serves 4

1 kilo veal leg or shoulder off the bone
2 tbsp olive oil
150 g panzetta
2 onions, chopped
1 tbsp plain flour
2 cloves garlic, crushed
4 carrots peeled and sliced thinly
1 tbsp tomato concentrate
1 bay leaf, 2 sprigs thyme, 1 sprig rosemary
3 glasses dry white wine
150 cl chicken or veal stock
salt and pepper
150 g green olives

Cut the veal into cubes of about 3 cms. Heat the oil in a heavy-bottomed casserole and, when it is very hot, quickly fry the pieces of veal on all sides to seal in all the juices. Remove with a slotted spoon and reserve. Add the *panzetta* and fry for a minute or two. Turn the heat down and fry the onions until they start to soften. Put the meat and any juices back into the pan and sprinkle with the flour. Cook and stir for a minute or two. Add the garlic, carrots, tomato concentrate and herbs. Stir again and add the wine and stock. Season with salt and pepper to taste (go easy on the salt because of the saltiness of the *panzetta*) and bring to the boil. Lower the heat and simmer, covered, for 45 minutes. Add the olives and adjust the seasoning if need be. Simmer for another 30 minutes and serve with pasta.

VEAL AND AUBERGINE STEW

Tianu di vitellu incu melizane Serves 4

1 kilo veal suitable for blanquettes
3 tbsp olive oil
1 large onion, chopped
2 cloves garlic, crushed and chopped
1 tbsp plain flour
½ litre dry white wine
1 bay leaf, 2 sprigs thyme
1 kilo aubergines
salt and pepper

Cut the veal into medium-sized pieces (about 4 cms square). Heat the oil in a heavy-bottomed casserole and fry the meat on all sides to seal in the juices. Remove with a slotted spoon and reserve. Lower the heat and fry the onion and garlic until it they soften. Stir in the flour and cook for a few minutes stirring constantly. Pour in the wine and add the meat pieces with any juice and the herbs. Stir in any crusty bits from the bottom of the casserole and season with salt and pepper. Add just enough hot water to cover the meat and bring to the boil before lowering the heat to simmer. Cook, covered, for one hour. Peel and cube the aubergines and add to the stew. Cook for a further 30 minutes. Correct seasoning and serve with pasta, rice or potatoes.

BEEF STEW

Stufatu Serves 6 to 8

This stew is sometimes referred to as a sauce in Corsica, probably because it is almost always served mixed with pasta. Any leftovers are used to flavour other dishes such as a stew of large white beans.

2 tbsp olive oil
1 $^{1}/_{2}$ kilos of lean beef cut into cubes
250 g cured ham or bacon in one piece (the end bits are cheapest)
24 pickling onions or 2 large onions cut into segments pole to pole
2 tbsp tomato concentrate
4 cloves garlic, crushed
2 glasses red wine
1 bay leaf, 1 sprig thyme, 1 sprig rosemary tied together
2 cloves
100 g dried porcini *or ceps*
salt and pepper

Heat the oil in a heavy-bottomed saucepan and, when it is very hot, brown the beef in small quantities, taking the pieces out with a slotted spoon and reserving them as you go along. Lower the heat and start cooking the ham. Add the onions and when they start to brown, add the tomato concentrate, garlic and the beef with any juices. Add the rest of the ingredients and enough water to cover. Bring to the boil and then lower the heat to simmer. Cover and cook over a very low heat for 2 $^{1}/_{2}$ to 3 $^{1}/_{2}$ hours, or until the beef is tender. Meanwhile, soak the *porcini* in warm water and add, drained, to the meat about one hour before the end of the cooking time. Rectify seasoning and serve with large pasta.

MEATBALLS

Pulpettes Serves 4

These meatballs can also be made with cooked meat left over from a roast or a stew.

200 g minced beef or wild boar
1 large onion, finely chopped
2 slices bread soaked in milk and squeezed dry
2 tbsp chopped parsley
1 beaten egg
2 tbsp plain flour
2 tbsp oil or lard
For the tomato sauce:
1 tbsp olive oil
1 onion, minced
2 cloves garlic, minced
1 tbsp tomato concentrate
5 ripe tomatoes, peeled and chopped or one tin chopped tomatoes
1 bay leaf, 1 sprig thyme
salt and pepper

Mix well together the minced meat, chopped onion, soaked breadcrumbs, chopped parsley and egg (use your hands), and form into spheres about the size of ping-pong balls. Roll them in the flour and fry them in the oil until browned all over. Make the tomato sauce as follows. Heat the oil gently in a saucepan and fry the onion until soft. Stir in the garlic and tomato concentrate and herbs. Cook for a minute or two and add the chopped tomatoes. Season with salt and pepper and simmer, covered, for 20 minutes. Put the meatballs in the sauce and simmer for 20 minutes more.

VEGETABLE DISHES, PASTA, AND SOME SAUCES

VEGETABLES

Until the end of the nineteenth century, the choice of vegetables in Corsica was very limited. Potatoes, tomatoes, cabbages, garlic, leeks, onions and beans, green in summer and dried in winter, were augmented by wild plants (chard and asparagus) and herbs. Dried chick-peas were also used, and lupin seeds which were cooked in the same way as lentils. Since the beginning of the twentieth century, and most of all since the First World War, other vegetables have made their appearance: peas, aubergines, courgettes, carrots, Brussels sprouts, cauliflowers, artichokes, peppers and, in the last few years, broccoli.

As you see from the following recipes, vegetables are rarely boiled but are grilled, baked, fried in batter or served in a sauce.

STUFFED ARTICHOKES

Artichiocci incu brocciu Allow 2 to 3 per person

The first artichokes of the season to arrive in the market are greeted with delight. Small and tender, they are sold in bunches of eight, and are whisked off to be served raw as a delicious light meal with olive oil and lemon, or stuffed with creamy *brocciu* and simmered in a tomato sauce. To make sure that you buy really fresh artichokes, check that the stalks are stiff and not limp. For this dish you will need small artichokes.

Prepare twelve small artichokes. Trim the stalks and take off the outer leaves. Cut the top half off the other leaves. As you finish each artichoke, put it in a bowl of water acidulated with the juice of a lemon to prevent it turning black. When they are all prepared, cook them in boiling salted water for 15 minutes. Let them cool slightly and, with a teaspoon, open the leaves out a little to make place for the stuffing. If they are young they will not have any chokes to remove.

For the stuffing:
400 g brocciu
2 slices ham, finely chopped
150 g grated hard Corsican cheese or gruyère
2 eggs
2 tbsp chopped parsley or mint
3 tbsp fresh breadcrumbs
50 g butter
salt and pepper

tomato sauce

Mix the first five ingredients together and stuff the artichokes. Make a tomato sauce as for the meatballs on page 152, adding a glass of white wine (if you like) at the same time as the tomatoes. Pour the sauce into an oven dish and sit the artichokes in one layer on top. Sprinkle with breadcrumbs and dot with butter. Cover the dish with aluminium foil and cook in a preheated oven (190°C/gas 5) for 30 minutes. Remove the foil and cook for a further 10 minutes until the tops are brown. Vegetarians can leave out the ham.

If necessary you can use larger artichokes. Just make sure that you cut the leaves right down to remove the tough parts. When they are cooked, you will need to remove the hairy choke from the middle. It is quite easy to do so using a teaspoon.

STUFFED AUBERGINES

Mirizani pieni Serves 6

In Bonifacio, near the southernmost tip of the island, this dish is always prepared for September 8, the Pilgrimage of the Trinity, the ham being replaced by four beaten eggs.

6 aubergines
For the stuffing:
300 g ham, chopped
100 g hard Corsican cheese, grated
1 tbsp chopped basil
1 tbsp chopped parsley
4 slices bread soaked in milk and squeezed out
2 cloves garlic, finely chopped
2 tbsp plain flour
salt and pepper
3 tbsp olive oil
tomato sauce as in the meatball recipe on page 152

Plunge the aubergines into boiling salted water for 10 minutes. Remove them and, when they have cooled slightly, cut them in half lenthways. Scoop out most of the flesh with a spoon, being careful not to split the skins, and chop it finely. Squeeze this chopped flesh dry of any surplus liquid in a clean cloth or kitchen paper, then mix it with the next seven ingredients. Fill the shells with this mixture and dust the tops with the flour. Fry the aubergines in the oil until they are golden on all sides. Pour the tomato sauce into an oven dish and place the aubergines on top. Cook in a preheated medium oven (200°C/gas 6) for 45 minutes.

AUBERGINE LASAGNE

Mirizani di lasagne Serves 6

4 large or 6 medium aubergines
sea salt
½ cup olive oil
tomato sauce as in previous recipes, but with double the amount of tomatoes
12 basil leaves, torn into pieces
100 g grated hard cheese

Take the stalks off the aubergines and cut into slices crosswise. Sprinkle them with sea salt and leave them to drain for 1 hour. Rinse and pat dry. Brush with the olive oil on both sides and grill or fry until golden and soft.

In a fairly deep oven dish, make alternate layers of aubergine and sauce, scattering the basil between, until you have used all the aubergines, finishing with a layer of sauce. Cook, covered, in a low oven (180°C/gas 4) for an hour until the aubergines are very soft. Remove the lid from the casserole, sprinkle with the cheese and bake for another 30 minutes.

AUBERGINES COOKED WITH TOMATOES

Mirizani incu a pummata Serves 4 to 6

4 large aubergines
4 large tomatoes
½ glass olive oil
6 cloves garlic, finely chopped
4 tbsp chopped mint
pinch of sugar
salt and pepper

Peel the aubergines, cut the flesh into dice about 2 centimetres square and sprinkle with salt. Leave for 30 minutes, rinse, squeeze, and pat dry with a clean towel or kitchen paper. Skin the tomatoes and deseed them. Dice the flesh. Heat the oil in a large frying-pan and fry the aubergines for 5 minutes, turning them 2 or 3 times. Add the garlic and mint and continue cooking for 1 or 2 minutes. Add the tomato cubes and sprinkle with the sugar. Cook all together, stirring carefully, for another 5 minutes. Season with pepper and add salt if necessary. Serve hot or cold.

STUFFED CEPS

Buledri pieni Serves 4

The ceps in this recipe can be replaced by field mushrooms, and the liver by ham.

100 g lamb's liver
1/2 glass red wine
4 large or 8 medium sized mushrooms (ceps for preference)
2 shallots
2 cloves garlic
2 tbsp olive oil
100 g fresh breadcrumbs
2 tbsp parsley, salt and pepper

Marinate the liver in the red wine for 12 hours. Drain. Wipe the mushrooms with a damp cloth and remove the stalks. Chop the shallots and garlic finely. Heat 1 tbsp of the oil in a frying-pan and fry the shallots and garlic gently until soft. Chop the mushroom stalks and liver finely and mix with the shallot and garlic mixture, breadcrumbs, parsley and salt and pepper. Stuff the mushroom heads with this mixture and place on an oiled baking tray. Sprinkle with the rest of the oil and bake in a preheated oven (200°C/gas 6) for 30 minutes.

COS LETTUCE STUFFED WITH BROCCIU

Insalata incu brocciu Serves 4

2 large or 4 small cos lettuces
400 g fresh brocciu
2 eggs, beaten
2 tbsp chopped basil or mint
1 clove garlic, crushed
1 tbsp olive oil, salt and pepper

Discard the outer leaves of the lettuces and, leaving them whole, rinse the rest under running cold water. Mash the *brocciu* and mix with the eggs and herbs. Season. If the hearts of the lettuce are very hard, remove and chop them and mix with the *brocciu*. Bring a saucepan of salted water to the boil and dip the lettuces in it briefly to soften them slightly. Cut the large lettuces in half lengthways. Put a spoonful of stuffing between each leaf and refold the lettuces together, tying them with fine string. Prop the lettuces up in a deep saucepan (an asparagus kettle is perfect) and pour in boiling water to come halfway up the lettuces. Add the garlic, a teaspoonful of salt and the olive oil. Cover the saucepan and cook the lettuces for 20 minutes. Remove the string and serve with a little of the juice. You can also cook the lettuces in a steamer, in which case serve with a little melted butter or heated cream.

CABBAGE STUFFED WITH FIGATELLU

Carbusgiu pienu incu figatellu

This recipe is infinitely variable. You can use any sort of meat: sausage, ham, chicken, pork, lamb, veal or meat from a left-over roast. You can substitute cheese for the meat if you prefer. You can cook the cabbage in stock or wine or a mixture of the two. Here I have used *figatellu*, the liver sausage beloved by Corsicans, to stuff the cabbage.

1 large Savoy cabbage
For the stuffing:
150 g panzetta
200 g figatellu
150 g fresh breadcrumbs soaked in milk for 10 minutes and squeezed dry
1 egg
2 tbsp chopped parsley
1 tsp chopped fresh thyme leaves or 1/2 tsp dried thyme
salt and pepper
For the sauce:
2 tbsp olive oil
1 onion, finely chopped
2 cloves garlic, crushed
2 tbsp tomato concentrate
1 bay leaf
1 hot red chilli pepper, deseeded
1 carrot, peeled and chopped

Remove the skin from the *figatellu* and chop up with the *panzetta*. Mix well with the other stuffing ingredients. Season, but don't use much salt as the meats are already salty. Remove the outer leaves and level the base of the cabbage. Bring a big pan of salted water to the boil and cook the cabbage in it for a few minutes, just enough to soften the leaves. Do not overcook it. Remove from the pan and plunge into cold water. When cool, drain. If the centre is very hard, remove it, chop it, and mix it with the stuffing. Gently pull the leaves apart and put some stuffing on each one. When you have used up the stuffing tie the cabbage back into shape.

Heat the oil in a large casserole or saucepan just big enough to hold the cabbage and gently fry the onion. When it has softened, add the garlic, tomato concentrate, bay leaf and red chilli pepper. Cook, stirring, for a couple of minutes and add the carrot and seasonings.

Put in the cabbage and add just enough water to almost cover it. Cover tightly and cook, very slowly, on top or in the oven (155°C/gas 2/3) for 2 to 2 ½ hours. This is a very good-tempered dish and if you cook it for a little longer it won't matter a bit. When you are ready to serve it, remove the string and cut the cabbage in wedges. Degrease the sauce and serve with the cabbage.

FENNEL GRATIN

Finochju a l'antica Serves 4

Fennel is frequently used in recipes to add flavour. The branches are added to wood fires when grilling fish, and the seeds have those overtones of the aniseed used to make *pastis*, the alcoholic drink most loved by Corsicans.

4 bulbs Florence fennel
2 tbsp olive oil or butter
2 tbsp plain flour
⅓ litre milk
2 eggs
100 g grated hard cheese
salt and pepper

Trim the fennel and cook in plenty of boiling salted water for 10 minutes. Drain. In a second pan, heat the oil or butter and stir in the flour. Gradually add the milk, whisking until it comes to the boil. Simmer for 10 minutes. Take it off the heat, let it cool slightly and then beat in the eggs. Stir in the cheese and season with salt and pepper. Cut the fennel bulbs in half lengthways and put into an oiled or buttered oven dish. Pour the sauce over and cook in a preheated oven (220°C/gas 7) for 20 minutes or until the cheese topping is golden brown.

GREEN BEANS AND LEEKS WITH TOMATO

U fasciolu e i porri a pumata Serves 6

1 kilo green beans (haricots verts)
4 leeks
2 tbsp olive oil
3 tbsp tomato purée or 4 ripe tomatoes, peeled and chopped
2 cloves garlic, crushed and chopped
1 bay leaf, salt and pepper

Top, tail and wash the beans, then break in half. Split and wash the leeks and cut into slices, using only the white parts. Heat the oil in a saucepan and gently cook the leeks and beans until the leeks start to soften. Add the tomato, bay leaf and garlic and enough water to barely cover. Season to taste, bring to the boil, then lower the heat and simmer for about 20 minutes, or until all the liquid has been absorbed. The acidity from the tomatoes will keep the beans nice and firm.

BROAD BEAN STEW

U tianu di fave freshe Serves 6

3 slices panzetta
2 tbsp olive oil
1 large onion, chopped
800 g podded broad beans
2 eggs, salt and pepper

Chop the *panzetta* and fry in the oil in a large frying-pan until turning golden. Add the onion and cook until it softens. Put in the beans and seasonings and enough hot water to cover. Simmer for about 20 minutes or until the water is absorbed. Beat the eggs and add them to the dish, stirring, until they are just set. Serve immediately.

COURGETTE FRITTERS

Fritelle de zucchini Serves 4

200 g plain flour
1 tsp baking powder
pinch salt
1 egg
330 ml water and/or milk
4 large or 6 small courgettes

Sift the flour, salt and baking powder into a bowl and make a well in the centre. Beat the egg slightly and stir into the flour with a fork, gradually working in the flour from the sides of the bowl. Add enough liquid to make a batter the consistency of cream. Cover with a cloth and leave to settle for about an hour. Top and tail the courgettes and cut them into slices about the thickness of a coin. Dip them into the batter and fry in fairly hot deep oil until golden brown. Drain on kitchen paper, sprinkle with salt if liked, and serve straight away. You can also grate the courgettes and mix them directly with the batter. Drop spoonfuls into the hot oil and serve as above. Alternatively, you can make them in the following manner.

COURGETTE GALETTES

Fritelle de zucchini Serves 6

1 kilo courgettes
plain flour
6 eggs
1 tbsp baking powder
salt and pepper

Grate the courgettes into a bowl. Add just enough flour to hold the courgettes together. Beat the eggs with the baking powder and plenty of salt and pepper and add to the courgettes. Mix well. Heat a little oil in a frying-pan and drop in spoonfuls of the mixture. Try one spoonful first and if it doesn't hold together well, add a little more flour. It is better to add more flour if need be than put in too much in the first place. Fry until golden, turning them once, and drain on kitchen paper.

COURGETTE CASSEROLE

Serves 6 as a side dish

1 kilo courgettes
1 large or 2 medium onions, preferably the sweet purple kind
2 tbsp olive oil
4 eggs
salt and pepper

Top and tail the courgettes and cut into fairly thin rounds. Chop the onions. Heat the oil in a large frying-pan and fry the courgettes and onions over a low heat, stirring, until turning brown. This will take about 15 minutes. Season well. Break the eggs into the pan and stir with a fork so that you get alternate yellow and white streaks. Serve immediately.

WHITE BEANS AND MUSHROOMS

Fascioli incu funghi Serves 6

Potatoes were not introduced into Corsica until the end of the eighteenth century. Until then, the main winter staples, apart from chestnuts, were pulses and beans. Chickpeas, lentils and several varieties of beans were all used, and lupins were eaten until the end of the nineteenth century. The seeds had to be soaked for three days in running water, usually the river, to rid them of their dangerous toxins. Even so, they still managed to give indigestion to those unfortunate or hungry enough to eat them. Beans and lentils, however, still provide a large part of the winter diet.

This dish would be made with the large white kidney beans called *soissons*, named for their region of origin in France.

250 g dried white kidney beans
125 g dried ceps or wild mushrooms
2 tbsp olive oil or lard
1 large onion, chopped
2 cloves garlic, crushed
2 tbsp tomato concentrate
2 bay leaves
salt and pepper

Soak the beans and mushrooms separately in cold water for 8 hours. Drain the beans, cover with fresh water and add salt. Bring to the boil and then lower heat and simmer for 1 to 1 $^{1}/_{2}$ hours. Meanwhile drain the mushrooms, straining and saving the liquid.

Heat the oil or lard in a thick-bottomed saucepan or oven-proof casserole. Cook the onion until it softens. Add the garlic, tomato concentrate, bay leaves and drained mushrooms and cook, stirring, for a couple of minutes. Season with salt and lots of ground pepper and add a wine-glass full of the reserved mushroom liquid. Add the beans and enough of their liquid to just cover, mix well and simmer, covered, either on top of the stove or in a preheated oven (190°C/gas 5) for 20 to 30 minutes. Add a little more of the reserved mushroom liquid or water if the beans seem to be drying out. The stew should be fairly liquid.

STUFFED ONIONS

E civolle pienu incu brocciu Serves 4

The onion is known as the king of vegetables in Corsica. Here is a delicious way of cooking it.

4 largish onions
250 g brocciu, *ricotta or cream cheese*
100 g prizuttu *(in England you could buy* coppa *or a* jambon de Bayonne*)*
1 egg
1 tbsp chopped parsley
2 tbsp olive oil
salt and pepper

Peel the onions and blanch them in boiling salted water for 3 minutes. Take out and let cool. Chop the ham and mix it with the *brocciu*, parsley, beaten egg and salt and pepper to taste. Cut off the top third of each onion and take out the inner leaves, leaving a thick outer casing. Fill with the cheese mixture and put the lids back on. Place in an oven dish and dribble with the olive oil. Cook in a preheated moderate oven (200°C/gas 6) for 35 to 40 minutes.

POTATO TARTS

Sciatta di pommi Makes 6 tarts

These tarts are a speciality of Levie, a village in the Alta Rocca in the south of the island. They are prepared for the 'Day of the Dead' on November 1 and 2.

2 cloves garlic, peeled
½ glass olive oil
500 g potatoes, boiled in their skins
150 g hard cheese, grated
½ tsp cayenne
salt and pepper
milk
300 g short-crust pastry

Heat the garlic with the oil and then allow to cool. Remove the garlic. Peel and mash the potatoes and mix with the oil and 100 grams of the cheese. Add enough milk to make the mash light and fluffy; season well with cayenne, salt and pepper. Roll out the short-crust pastry on a lightly floured board and, using a small saucer as a guide, cut out 6 rounds of about 14 centimetres diameter. Place these on a baking tray and divide the potato mix between them, putting some in the centre of each round and spreading it to 2 cm from the edges. Pull the pastry up all around to make a purse, pinching it with your fingertips to hold it together. Sprinkle the tops with the rest of the cheese and bake in a preheated oven (200°C/gas 6) for about 45 minutes. In other parts of the island the cayenne pepper is replaced with a handful of chopped mint. These are very good served hot or cold, either on their own, or in place of a vegetable.

POTATO AND TOMATO BAKE

Testu Serves 4 to 6

The success of this very simple recipe, from the village of Alata, just outside Ajaccio, depends on the quality and ripeness of the tomatoes. It is a dish to make in summer when they are (hopefully) sweet and juicy with sunshine.

1 kilo potatoes
1 kilo ripe tomatoes
100 ml olive oil, salt and pepper

Peel and slice the potatoes thinly. Slice the tomatoes thickly. Put them in alternate layers in a well-oiled baking dish, seasoning each layer as you go. Finish with tomatoes. Use plenty of pepper. Pour the oil evenly over the top and bake in a medium to hot oven (210°C/gas 6/7) for 1 to 1½ hours.

CHICKPEA SALAD

Insalata di ceci Serves 4

250 g chickpeas
1 tbsp bicarbonate of soda
1 bunch spring onions
1 tbsp French mustard
1 tbsp wine vinegar
3 tbsp chopped parsley
2 cloves garlic, finely chopped
4 tbsp olive oil, salt and pepper

Soak the chickpeas overnight with the bicarbonate of soda. Drain and rinse and cook in salted water for 1 hour or until tender. Strain and cool. Finely chop the onions. Mix the mustard and vinegar with salt and pepper to taste and beat in the oil. Mix in the onion, garlic, parsley and chickpeas.

CHICKPEA FLOUR TARTLETS
Panizze

Panizze are very popular in Bastia, the largest town on the east coast, and are undoubtedly first cousins to the *panisse* which are sold in Nice and which originate in the Italian mainland, just 82 kilometres away. They are sold in the markets or by street vendors.

1 litre water
300 g chickpea flour
salt and pepper, sunflower oil

Bring 1 litre of salted water to the boil and pour in the chickpea flour, whisking all the time. Cook until it has thickened, about 40 minutes, stirring with a wooden spoon from time to time to stop any lumps forming. Oil several small ramekins or a shallow dish and pour in the *panizze*. Either eat it hot as it is with oil and pepper or let it cool, cut it into thin slices and fry the slices. You can sprinkle these with sugar or salt and pepper. You can also cook the *panizze*, cut into thickish slices, in a well-flavoured tomato and basil sauce.

CHICKPEA FLOUR FRITTERS
Panzarotti incu farina di ceci

10 g fresh yeast
150 g plain flour
50 g chickpea flour
1 tbsp olive oil
1/2 liqueur glass eau de vie *(or other liqueur)*
pinch salt
2 eggs
grated rind of 1/2 lemon

Mix the yeast with a little warm water and leave for 10 minutes until it starts to froth. Sift into the yeast the flours and salt. Add the oil and *eau de vie* and enough cold water to make a batter the consistency of a thick cake mix. Cover and leave to rise in a warm place for 1 hour. Separate the eggs and add the yolks to the batter with the lemon rind, beating well. Beat the egg whites with a pinch of salt until stiff and fold into the batter. Fry spoonfuls of the batter in deep fat until golden and drain on kitchen paper. Dredge with sugar before serving.

OLIVES

Wild olive trees are part of the *maquis*, the fragrant undergrowth of shrubs and trees that covers two-thirds of the island. In most Mediterranean countries olives are gathered by putting nets under the trees and shaking or beating the tree until the olives fall into them. Corsicans joke that they take this one stage further by putting the nets under the trees and waiting until the olives fall into them of their own accord! In fact, this means that the olives are riper and give rounder, sweeter tasting oil of a very high quality. Olive oil labelled as 'fruity' is made from fruit that is not quite ripe and that still has chlorophyll in it. From the end of the eighteenth century, when large quantities of oil were exported, the olive oil trade had practically disappeared but is now enjoying a resurgence, thanks to the initiative of a group of professional producers.

TOMATOES STUFFED WITH OLIVES

Pumate pienu incu l'alvie Serves 4

4 large ripe tomatoes
1 bunch spring onions or 1 medium salad onion
200 g black olives
2 tbsp chopped parsley
100 ml olive oil
salt and pepper

Slice the tops off the tomatoes and empty them out with a teaspoon. Chop the white parts of the spring onion, or the onion, finely. Stone the olives and chop coarsely. Mix with the onion, parsley and olive oil and season well. Stuff the tomatoes carefully with this mixture and serve chilled as a first course.

PASTA

PASTA WITH MEAT SAUCE

Pasta asciuta Serves 4

This is the most popular everyday Corsican dish, served for lunch in countless homes all over the island.

500 g boneless beef, lamb or veal
2 tbsp olive oil
2 medium onions, chopped
2 cloves garlic, crushed and chopped
2 tbsp tomato concentrate
1 bay leaf, 1 sprig thyme, 1 sprig rosemary
salt and pepper
500 g dried pasta (macaroni or rigoni)
150 g grated hard cheese

Cut the meat of your choice into pieces about 2 centimetres square. Heat the oil in a large saucepan and fry the meat over a high heat until it is brown all over. Remove and put to one side. Lower the heat and fry the onions until they soften. Add the garlic and tomato and cook, stirring, for two minutes. Put back the meat and any juices and the herbs. Cover with water and bring to the boil. Season with salt and pepper and simmer until meat is tender. The time will vary depending on which meat you use: beef will take about 2 hours, lamb 1 ½ hours and veal 1 hour. Blanch the pasta in boiling water for 3 minutes. Add to the stew and continue cooking until done, adding a little water if necessary. Put a layer of pasta and meat sauce in a dish and sprinkle with some of the cheese. Continue layering pasta and cheese until you have used all the pasta, finishing with the cheese. Serve. You can brown the dish under the grill if you like but this is not generally done in Corsica.

SWISS CHARD AND CHEESE DUMPLINGS

Storza preti Makes 4 starters or 2 main dishes

These dumplings or quenelles come from the town of Bastia on the east coast. It is said that the dish was invented by two sisters who kept a boarding house for priests. One evening they discovered that they had run out of pasta to cook the stuffed canelloni that they were going to serve for dinner and improvised by turning the stuffing into these little dumplings. Their lodgers complimented them on the dish and, on being asked the name of it, the sisters charmingly replied ‘Storza preti’ which means ‘Smothered priests’.

They are usually served covered with the sauce from the meat dish with which they are to be served, topped with cheese and browned in the oven. You can also serve them with a cheese or tomato sauce. When making them it is important to squeeze out all the moisture from the greens and chop them very finely. They are quite delicate and difficult to handle at first but are well worth the effort.

750 g Swiss chard (green leaves only)
2 tbsp fresh herbs (choose from mint, basil, parsley or half the amount of marjoram)
250 g brocciu, *ricotta or cream cheese*
2 large or 3 small eggs
salt and pepper
flour
grated hard cheese

Cook the chard in a little salted water for 10 minutes and drain. Squeeze out all moisture using a cloth or kitchen paper, mix with the herbs and chop finely. Crush the cheese with a fork, beat the eggs and seasonings and mix together with the greens. Refrigerate to allow it to settle for at least 30 minutes. Generously flour a board and gently roll the cheese mixture into a sausage shape about 3 centimetres thick. Don't worry if it's uneven. Cut into three-centimetre lengths. These you now make into balls. Put a little flour into a wine glass and add one of the stubby cheese and chard sausages. Holding the glass by the stem, rotate it very quickly so that the cheese spins round to form a floured ball. (Try it, it really does work!) Do this with all the other pieces, putting them on a lightly floured plate as you finish each one. Bring a large shallow pan of salted water to the boil and then turn down the heat so that it just simmers. Add the cheese balls very carefully, one at a time. Do not crowd the pan. When they float to the surface they are cooked. Take them out with a slotted spoon and put them in a shallow, buttered oven dish. Cover them with a sauce of your choice: meat, tomato or cheese. Sprinkle with grated cheese and cook in a preheated oven (220°C/gas 7) until the cheese topping is nicely browned.

CHEESE RAVIOLI

Panzarotti incu brocciu

Pasta owes its existence in Corsica to the Genoese occupation and has been produced locally since before the early nineteenth century. Ravioli is usually stuffed with fresh *brocciu* which is sometimes mixed with Swiss chard as in this recipe.

For the pasta:
400g plain flour
3 small or 2 large eggs
cold water
pinch of salt

For the stuffing:
250 g Swiss chard
300 g brocciu, *ricotta or cream cheese*
2 eggs
1 tbsp chopped mint or nepita *(calamint)*
salt and pepper

Sieve the flour and salt together and make a well in the centre. Add the eggs gradually, working in the flour from the sides. Knead the dough and, if necessary, add a little cold water, just enough to make a soft elastic dough. Leave the dough to rest for half an hour. Cook the green leaves of the Swiss chard (use the stalks for some other dish) in a little salted water until tender, about 10 minutes. Drain very well, squeezing out any moisture with your hands, and chop finely together with the mint or *nepita*. By this time the chard should be cool. Beat the eggs and crush the *brocciu* with a fork. Mix them into the greens and season well with salt and pepper.

Divide the dough into two equal parts and roll out on a floured surface into thin square or rectangular sheets of roughly the same size. Put teaspoonfuls of the filling at equal distances from each other on one piece of dough. Use your finger or a pastry brush to dab water between the fillings to form a grid of straight lines. Cover with the second sheet of dough and cut between the ravioli. Pinch the edges of the dough together with your fingers and put the ravioli on to a lightly floured plate.

Cook in simmering salted water for 4 to 5 minutes – the time depends on the thickness of the dough. Serve with a tomato or cheese sauce, or layered with a grated hard cheese and topped with a light meat sauce.

SWISS CHARD CANNELLONI

Pasta incu bietulle Serves 4 to 6

These cannelloni seem complicated to make but are just a bit time-consuming. You could prepare the dish up to the stage of putting it into the oven the day before you want to serve it. You can substitute *brocciu* for the white sauce.

400 g Swiss chard
2 tbsp butter or olive oil
2 tbsp plain flour
½ litre milk
1 bay leaf
1 clove garlic, chopped
1 tbsp chopped mint
salt and pepper
16 sheets lasagne

Strip then wash the green leaves of the chard and cook in a little salted water for five minutes. Drain well and chop finely. Peel off the transparent outer skin of the stalks and dice them. Cook in boiling salted water for 10 minutes. Drain. Melt the butter or heat the oil in a small saucepan and stir in the flour. Cook until pale beige. Add the milk a little at a time, stirring all the while to eliminate lumps. Bring to the boil and lower heat. Add the bay leaf, chopped garlic, mint and seasonings. Cook for 5 minutes, stirring from time to time. Remove bay leaf. Mix the chard and sauce together.

Cook the lasagne in plenty of boiling salted water until they float to the surface. Take out with a slotted spoon and plunge into cold water. Drain on a clean tea cloth or kitchen paper. Spoon some filling on to each one, roll them up and put into a buttered oven dish, in rows. Spoon any left-over sauce between them. Cover with tomato sauce and sprinkle with grated cheese. Cook in a hot oven (225°C/gas 7/8) for 20 minutes or until the cheese topping has browned.

Tomato sauce:
1 onion, chopped
1 tbsp olive oil
1 clove garlic, chopped
1 tbsp tomato concentrate
4 or 5 ripe tomatoes, peeled and chopped, or 1 tin chopped tomatoes
1 bay leaf, 1 sprig thyme
salt and pepper

Fry the onion in the oil until it softens and add the garlic and tomato paste. Stir for a minute or two and add the tomatoes, herbs and salt and pepper. Simmer, covered, for 20 minutes.

SOME SAUCES

PEVERONATA SAUCE

A salsa piverunata

The recipe for this sauce comes from Corte, an ancient fortress town in the centre of Corsica. It is supposed to have been introduced by Lord Byron when he stayed there.

3 tbsp olive oil
1 thick slice panzetta, *cubed*
1 large onion, chopped
2 red or green peppers, seeded and diced
2 cloves garlic, crushed
4 tomatoes, peeled, seeded and chopped
1 bay leaf
½ litre red wine
salt and pepper

Heat the oil in a wide pan and fry the *panzetta* until the fat is translucent. Add the onion and start cooking gently until it starts to wilt. Add the peppers and garlic and continue cooking, stirring, for 2 or 3 minutes. Add the tomatoes, bay leaf and wine and about 150 ml of water. Bring to the boil and then reduce heat and simmer, covered, for half an hour. Season to taste. Serve with eggs, fish or meat.

VINAIGRETTE WITH ANCHOVIES

A salsa incu anchiuve

6 salted anchovies or 12 fillets in oil
3 tbsp olive oil
1 tbsp wine vinegar
½ tsp freshly ground black pepper

Pound in a mortar, or you can crush them with the flat of a knife, some ready-prepared fillets of anchovies or washed salted anchovies, with their fillets prised off. Heat the oil and cook the anchovies for 1 minute. Add the vinegar and pepper and leave to cool slightly. Serve over salad, particularly a salad containing bitter leaves like dandelion or rocket.

ANOTHER TOMATO SAUCE

A salsa pumate

1 onion, finely chopped
2 tbsp olive oil
2 cloves garlic, finely chopped
1 tbsp tomato concentrate
5 ripe tomatoes, peeled, seeded and chopped (or 1 tin chopped tomatoes)
salt and pepper

Cook the onion in the oil until soft and then add the garlic and tomato concentrate. Stir and cook for a minute or two and add the tomatoes, salt and pepper. Cover and simmer for 20 minutes, stirring from time to time to stop the sauce sticking to the bottom of the pan. This sauce is used extensively in Corsican cooking and is often flavoured with herbs such as marjoram, thyme or basil. For a hot sauce, add a small hot red chilli pepper, which is removed before serving.

GARLIC SAUCE

Agliata ou agliolu

5 fat cloves garlic
5 tbsp olive oil
½ glass white wine vinegar
1 bay leaf, 1 sprig thyme, 1 sprig rosemary
salt and pepper

Crush and chop the garlic and cook for a minute in the olive oil. Add the other ingredients and reduce the sauce by half. This sauce is usually poured over fried fish, which is then allowed to get cold before eating.

CHESTNUTS

Until the middle of the twentieth century, chestnuts formed such an important part of the Corsican diet that the chestnut tree was known as the bread tree. Corsicans could claim with pride that they could live on '*pane di lego e vino di petra*' meaning 'bread from wood [chestnut flour] and wine from stone [water]'. Even in times of hardship and famine the chestnut was readily available to be gathered, dried in the upper stories of the houses by the smoke of the open chimney (*fucone*), and ground into flour. The flour was used to make a variety of sweet and savoury dishes (at one famous wedding in the early nineteenth century, twenty-two different dishes made with chestnut flour were served). Among these would have been *pisticcini*, small flat breads cooked in the wood-fired oven, *fritelle*, fritters, and *nicci*, little cakes cooked on chestnut leaves.

Chestnuts were boiled, dried, smoked and roasted. Children in the mountains carried hot chestnuts in their pockets on the way to school on cold winter mornings, and travellers carried a few dried chestnuts to sustain them on their way. On All Saints' Day, boiled chestnuts were made into necklaces called *curoni* or *cudagne* for the children to wear and eat all day long.

Chestnut trees still cover large areas of the island, particularly the beautiful forests of Castagniccia and Bocagnano – where the annual chestnut fair is held in December. After falling into disuse, the chestnut flour mills are once again in production and the flour is available commercially. Enterprising young Corsicans have started experimenting and manufacturing new versions of biscuits and cakes that are lighter in texture and more acceptable to modern tastes than the rather heavy traditional confections. Chestnut flour should always be sifted before use. As it hasn't been treated with insecticides it is also best to store it in the fridge to discourage mites.

PULENDA

500 g chestnut flour
1 litre water

Bring the water to the boil in a very large saucepan and pour in the flour in a steady stream, stirring all the time with a strong wooden spoon. This has been likened to mixing cement and in Corsica the wooden handle of a broom was often used to do the stirring. I have found that with these proportions of flour to water it is not that difficult. When the mixture starts to come away from the sides of the saucepan the *pulenda* is ready. Turn it out onto a clean cloth which has been sprinkled with a little flour or on to a floured board. The *pulenda* is traditionally cut with a sort of cheese wire, but I've found that a knife works well enough. Cut into wedges and serve with *brocciu* and *figatellu* for a really Corsican meal, or with any sort of stew. Any left over *pulenda* can be sliced and fried. Indeed, it can be treated as you would polenta, the Italian version made with maize, of which *pulenda* is undoubtedly the original.

CHESTNUT FLOUR AND BACON

Maccaredda

1 thick slice panzetta
1 tbsp olive oil
300 g chestnut flour
½ litre water
salt

Cut the *panzetta* into cubes and cook in the oil in a frying-pan until the fat is translucent. Mix the flour and a pinch of salt with the water, whisking well to eliminate any lumps. Pour this over the panzetta in the pan and cook over a low heat for about 15 minutes, stirring the mixture all the time to prevent it sticking to the bottom of the pan.

CHESTNUT FLOUR PASTA

Pasta di castagna

250 g plain flour
200 g chestnut flour
½ tsp salt
4 eggs
1 tbsp olive oil

Sift the flours and salt into a large bowl and make a well in the centre. Beat the eggs and oil together and add to the flours gradually, stirring the flours in from the sides.

Knead well until the dough is elastic. Flour a board and roll out the dough thinly, or put the dough through a pasta-making machine. Cut into required shapes. Cook in plenty of boiling salted water for 5 minutes. This pasta goes very well with any sort of game or other meat that is cooked in a sauce. It can also be used in the ravioli recipe on page 175.

CHESTNUT FLOUR AND MILK

Serves 2

This preparation, called *brillulis* in the north and *granahjoli* in the south of the island, was eaten for breakfast in the winter. I'm sure it is still the case, though cornflakes have probably replaced it in many homes.

½ litre water
pinch salt
100 g chestnut flour, sifted
full-cream milk, preferably goat's milk

Bring the salted water to the boil and add the flour in a stream, whisking all the time. Lower heat and keep stirring for about 10 to 15 minutes, or until the mixture has darkened and thickened. Pour into two bowls and add as much milk, cold or hot, as you like. You could add some chestnut honey too.

BOILED CHESTNUTS
Balotte

Chestnuts are often cooked with fennel which grows wild on the island. The two tastes seem to marry well.

1 kilo chestnuts
1 tbsp salt
2 or 3 branches of fennel

Cover the chestnuts and fennel with salted water in a saucepan. Bring to the boil and simmer until the chestnuts are soft, about an hour. As soon as they are cool enough to handle make a small slit in them with a sharp pointed knife and press out the flesh. Keep the unpeeled chestnuts warm while you work as they are more difficult to peel when they are cold.

CHESTNUT FLOUR CAKE

Cake di castagna

150 g soft butter
175 g sugar
3 eggs
100 g plain flour
75 g chestnut flour
2 tbsp cornflour
2 tsp baking powder
pinch of salt
3 tbsp hot water
100 g walnut or hazelnut pieces

Cream the butter and sugar together either by hand with a wooden spoon (hard work) or in a mixer. Add the eggs one by one and beat really well. This step is important if your cake is going to be light. Sift together the flours, baking powder and salt, and gently fold this and the hot water alternately into the egg mixture. Also fold in the nut pieces, saving a few nice pieces to decorate the top. Line a cake tin with buttered greaseproof paper and fill with the cake mix. Decorate with the reserved nuts. Cook in a preheated oven (190°C/gas 5) for 40 to 45 minutes, or until a skewer inserted in the centre of the cake comes out clean. Leave to cool on a cake rack. Wrap in tinfoil to store.

You can vary this recipe by adding raisins or chopped candied fruit. Dredge them in flour before you add them to the mix: this will stop them sinking to the bottom.

CHESTNUT FLOUR FLAN

Pastizzu castagninu

1 vanilla pod
150 g chestnut flour
$^{1}/_{2}$ litre milk
4 eggs
100 g sugar

Split the vanilla pod lengthways and scrape out the seeds. Whisk the flour into the milk and bring to the boil. Add the pod and the seeds to the milk and cook gently for 2 minutes, stirring all the time. Leave to stand for 5 minutes. Meanwhile beat the eggs and 50 grams of the sugar together. Add to the chestnutty milk mixture and take out the vanilla pod. (Save it to use again.) Put the other 50 grams of sugar and the same quantity of water into a small saucepan and cook, without stirring, until it turns pale brown. Pour this into the bottom of a heatproof dish, twisting and turning to spread it out evenly; pour the chestnut flour mix on top. Put the flan dish into a baking tray and pour in enough warm water to come halfway up the side. Cook in a preheated oven (220°C/gas 7) for 35 to 40 minutes, or until set. Leave to get cold and turn out onto a plate. (Hold the plate over the top and invert the flan.) Serve cold.

The next two recipes aren't traditional, but I've included them because they're so nice.

CHESTNUT, RAISIN AND APPLE FLAPJACKS

Makes 12 to 15

These chestnut-flour flapjacks make a nice change for a special breakfast and are good eaten with bacon or chipolatas, or simply with butter and honey or jam.

60 g plain flour
60 g chestnut flour
2 tsp baking powder
pinch salt
1 egg
2 tbsp sugar
½ litre milk
½ cup raisins
1 apple

Sift the flours, baking powder and salt into a bowl and make a well in the centre. Break the egg into the centre and gradually work into the flour with the sugar. Add half the milk and beat until smooth. Cover and leave to stand for 1 hour. Meanwhile soak the raisins in a little hot water for half an hour and then strain. Peel and grate the apple. Add these to the batter with enough extra milk to make it the consistency of cake mix. Heat a griddle or frying-pan to a medium heat and wipe it with a cloth or kitchen paper which you have dipped in oil. Drop tablespoonfuls of the mixture onto the hot surface. Cook until bubbles begin to appear on the top and then flip them over to cook the other side. Stack them up as they are cooked and keep them warm, either in a low oven or covered with a clean cloth.

CHESTNUT FLOUR MUFFINS

Makes 12 muffins

140 g plain flour
140 g chestnut flour
2 ½ tsp baking powder
30 g caster sugar
½ tsp salt
1 egg
230 ml milk
60 g butter, melted and cooled slightly

Grease 12 muffin tins or use paper cases. Sift together the dry ingredients into a large bowl. In a second bowl whisk together the egg, milk and melted butter. Combine with the dry ingredients, mixing with a spoon just until all the flour is incorporated. Do not over-mix. Spoon into the tins or cases. Bake in a preheated oven (200°C/gas 6) for about 20 minutes or until springy to the touch. Cool slightly before serving with butter and jam or with chestnut jam.

CHESTNUT FLOUR SOUFFLÉ

Suffiate di castagne Serves 4

100 g chestnut flour
60 g sugar
60 g butter
2 eggs plus 2 extra egg whites
1 tbsp vanilla flavouring (or brandy, eau de vie *or rum)*
1 tbsp grated zest of lemon

Put the milk in a saucepan and whisk in the flour. Bring to the boil, whisking from time to time, and add the butter cut into pieces. Take off the heat and blend in the sugar, lemon, flavouring of your choice, and egg yolks. Whisk the egg whites with a pinch of salt until they are stiff and gently fold them into the mixture with a spoon. Turn into a buttered soufflé dish. Bake in a preheated moderate oven (200°C/gas 6) for 45 minutes. Serve immediately.

CHESTNUT FLOUR PANCAKES

Nicci di farina castagnina

For the pancakes:
75 g chestnut flour
75 g plain flour
1 egg
1 tbsp sugar
pinch salt
½ litre milk

For the filling:
4 tbsp runny honey
4 tbsp eau de vie *(or other liqueur)*
200 g brocciu

Sift the flours and salt into a bowl and stir in the sugar. Make a well in the centre and stir in the egg. Gradually add the milk, stirring in the flour from the sides, and beat well to get rid of any lumps. The batter should be the consistency of single cream. If it is too thick, add a little more milk or water. Leave to stand for 30 minutes. Crush the *brocciu* with a fork and mix with the honey and the *eau de vie*. Make the pancakes in the usual way keeping them warm on a covered plate as you make them. Divide the *brocciu* mixture between the pancakes and roll them up. Drizzle a little honey over them and serve warm. If you prefer, mix only half of the *eau de vie* with the *brocciu* and flame the finished pancakes with the rest before serving.

PUFFY CHESTNUT FRITTERS

Fritelle castagnine suffiate

40 g chestnut flour
20 g plain flour
60 g butter
pinch salt
3 eggs
oil for frying

Sift the flours and salt together. Melt the butter in a saucepan and stir in the flours and salt. Cook, stirring continuously, for a minute or two, until the mixture leaves the side of the pan. Remove from the heat and beat in the eggs one by one. This is like making choux pastry with plain wheat flour. Drop spoonfuls of this mixture into hot, but not smoking oil and cook the fritters until golden brown. Drain on kitchen paper and serve dredged with sugar.

CHESTNUT FLOUR TART

Torta castagnina

300 g chestnut flour
pinch of salt, 1 tbsp oil
150 g walnut pieces

Sift the flour and salt and mix with enough water to make a thick batter. Add the oil and walnuts and pour into a buttered pie or tart dish. Bake in a preheated fairly hot oven (220°C/ gas 7) for 15 to 20 minutes.

The above is a traditional recipe that keeps the pure taste of the chestnuts. It is also rather heavy and flat so here is a more modern, lighter version.

200 g chestnut flour
100 g plain flour
150 g walnut pieces
1 tbsp oil
3 tsp baking powder
pinch of salt
water to mix
butter for tart dish

Sift the flours, salt and baking powder and mix with enough water to make a thick batter. Add the oil, walnuts and sugar and pour into a buttered pie or tart dish. Bake in a preheated fairly hot oven (220°C/gas 7) for 15 to 20 minutes.

You can add raisins to either version.

CHESTNUT JAM

A confiturra di castagne

1 kilo peeled chestnuts
1 kilo sugar
200 ml water
1 vanilla pod

You will need a little more than a kilo of chestnuts in their shell to have a kilo of purée. Make a little cut on the flat side of each chestnut and cook in boiling salted water for 15 minutes. Drain and cool slightly and remove the two skins. Put the chestnuts through a vegetable mill or processor. Weigh the resultant purée. Make a syrup of the same weight of sugar and 200 ml water by boiling them together for 10 minutes. Add the chestnut purée. Slit the vanilla pod lengthways and add to the pan. Simmer gently for 30 minutes. Remove vanilla pod, put jam into sterilized pots and cover with rounds of greaseproof paper. Stretch clingfilm over the tops of the jars to seal. Label the jars when they have cooled.

SWEET DISHES AND BISCUITS

In most households, desserts would not have been served every day of the week but would have been reserved for special meals on feast days or religious festivals, or maybe on Sundays when other members of the family visited.

FIADONE

Brocciu is used in many Corsican desserts. This is the most popular and best known of them all.

4 eggs
150 g sugar
500 g brocciu, *ricotta or cream cheese*
grated rind of 1 lemon

Beat the eggs and sugar together until fluffy. Crush the *brocciu* with a fork and beat into the egg mixture together with the lemon zest. Pour into a well-greased oven dish and bake in a fairly hot oven (220°C/gas 7) for 30 minutes, or until a knife tip inserted in the middle comes out clean.

Sometimes the *fiadone* is cooked in a pastry case. If the mixture is cooked in individual pastry cases they will take about 20 minutes to cook. They are called *imbrucciate*.

FALCULELLE

Chestnut leaves were used in cooking the way we use aluminium foil or greaseproof paper, to prevent foodstuffs from burning or sticking. You will see these charming little cakes for sale in most cake or bread shops. The flavour of the chestnut leaves gives a very special taste.

2 eggs
75 g sugar
grated zest of $^1/_2$ *lemon (not waxed)*
2 tbsp plain flour
250 g brocciu
1 egg yolk
dried or fresh sweet chestnut leaves (don't forget that the horse chestnut or conker tree is not where all these chestnuts come from) which have been soaked in cold water for 1 hour

Beat the eggs and sugar together until fluffy and stir in the flour and lemon zest. Crush the *brocciu* with a fork and mix with the egg mixture. Leave to stand for 30 minutes. Place a spoonful of the mixture on each chestnut leaf and bake in a preheated medium oven (200°C/gas 6) for 10 minutes. Take out and brush the tops with the egg yolk. Replace in the oven and cook for a further 10 to 15 minutes.

CACCAVELLU

This brioche or cake, made in the form of a ring and garnished with eggs, is served at Easter. There should be as many eggs as members of the family. It has many different names, which vary according to the region: *campanile*, *cruconi* or *caccavellu* are three.

500 g plain flour
20 g fresh yeast
50 cl warm water
pinch of salt
125 g sugar
2 eggs
1 liqueur glass of eau de vie *(or other liqueur)*
50 g butter
1 tbsp pastis *(optional)*
4 hard-boiled eggs
eggwash

Sift the flour. Mix the yeast with the warm water and 100 g of the flour and let it rise in a warm place for 30 minutes. Mix with the rest of the flour, the salt, sugar and 2 eggs, the *eau de vie*, butter and *pastis* and knead energetically for 5 minutes. Cover with a plastic bag or a clean cloth and leave to rise in a warm place for two hours, or until well risen. Knead again and shape into one ring, or you can make two concentric rings, saving a little of the dough to attach the eggs. If you roll this remaining dough into thin strips, you can place each egg on the ring and stick it in place by means of two strips in the form of a cross – rather like two pieces of sticking plaster. Beat the remaining egg and brush the tops of the rings with it. Leave to rise, covered, in a warm place, for about 30 minutes, or until well risen, and cook in a preheated hot oven (220°C/gas 7) for 35 to 40 minutes.

CACCAVELLU WITH BROCCIU

Caccavellu incu brocciu

dough as in preceding recipe
for the filling:
200 g brocciu
50 g sugar
2 eggs
1 liqueur glass eau de vie *(optional)*
grated rind of 1 orange or lemon (non-waxed)

Follow the recipe for making the dough for *caccavellu* that I have already given. Once it has undergone the first rise, roll out the dough on a lightly floured board to form a circle about the size of a pizza for one person. Crush the *brocciu* with a fork and mix with the other ingredients, using only one of the eggs. Cut a hole in the middle of the dough so that it now looks like a life-preserver or lifebuoy, or a mint with a hole. Spread the cheese mixture round the centre of the ring you have formed and cover it by bringing the outsides of the dough over towards the centre. You can seal the edges together by wetting the dough before pinching it with your fingers. It must be well sealed. Beat the second egg and brush the top, then leave to rise before cooking as I have already explained.

FRIED BISCUITS

I frappi

Frappe, sometimes called *oreillettes* (ears) or *merveilles* (marvels) are traditionally served at every sort of festivity: elections, carnivals and (above all) weddings. There are many variations: whole eggs are sometimes used, the butter is replaced with lard, or no fat used at all. The biscuits can be flavoured with orange, lemon, aniseed or orange flour water.

2 egg yolks
80 g sugar
250 g plain flour
25 g melted butter
1 tsp baking powder
grated rind of 1 orange or lemon (unwaxed)
3 tbsp orange flower water
150 ml water

Beat the egg yolks and sugar together until fluffy and then add the rest of the ingredients. Mix together, using enough of the water to make a stiff dough. Knead until the pastry doesn't stick to your fingers and form into a ball. Cover with a cloth and leave to settle in a warm place for 2 hours. Lightly flour a board and roll out the pastry to the thickness of a coin. Using a ravioli cutter or a small knife, cut the pastry into lozenge shapes. Either twist them in the middle to form 'ears' or make a small cut lengthways in the centre of each one. Fry in medium hot, deep fat until golden, turning them once, drain on kitchen paper and serve dredged with sugar. They can be served hot or cold and will keep quite well in an airtight container, although they are nicer fresh.

FRITTERS

No celebration in Corsica is complete without *beignets* or fritters. Weddings, christenings, town hall functions, art gallery openings, confirmations, Prefectorial parties, elections, birthdays, feast days and saints' days. Even at open-air fairs you will find someone flicking gobs of batter into a pan of boiling fat and selling the resultant golden *fritelles*, drenched with sugar, for a few francs a dozen.

The batter can be made with wheat flour or chestnut flour, or a mixture of both. For festive occasions the fritters are often flavoured with lemon, orange, aniseed or *eau de vie,* and are sometimes stuffed with *brocciu* before being sprinkled with sugar.

I watched an elderly lady making *fritelles* at one of the many fairs held in the mountain villages. She scooped up some batter, squished it out between the forefinger and thumb of one hand and plucked it off and dropped it into a pot of boiling oil with the other at the rate of about 100 a minute. Do not try this at home. You can get just as good results using a teaspoon.

Apart from celebrations, *beignets* are served as part of a meal and can be stuffed with vegetables or fish. Sometimes yeast or baking powder is used in the batter, or egg whites are beaten and folded in at the last minute. Here are some recipes for every occasion.

RICE FRITTERS

Panzarotti Makes 20 to 30 fritters

100 g pudding rice
10 g dried yeast
3 eggs
250 g plain flour
pinch salt
2 tbsp sugar
1 tbs olive oil
grated rind of 1 lemon (unwaxed)
2 tbsp eau de vie *or other liqueur (optional)*

Wash the rice and cook it in either water or milk for 15 minutes. Drain and leave to cool. Sprinkle the yeast on to 2 tablespoonfuls warm water and a teaspoon of sugar in a small bowl and leave to rise in a warm place. Separate the eggs. Sift the flour and salt into a large bowl and mix with the oil, sugar, lemon rind and/or *eau de vie*, egg yolks, rice and risen yeast. Mix well and add just enough cold water to make a thickish batter the consistency of gloss paint in the tin or single cream. Cover with a cloth and leave in a warm place to rise for at least 1 hour. Beat the egg whites with a pinch of salt until they are stiff and fold carefully into the mixture. Drop spoonfuls of the mixture into a pan of hot, but not smoking, deep fat. Do not crowd the pan. When the fritters are golden brown underneath, flip them over and cook the other side. Drain on paper towels and dredge with sugar. Serve hot or cold.

BROCCIU FRITTERS

Fritelle incu brocciu

10 g dried yeast, a pinch of sugar
250 g plain flour
pinch salt
1 large or 2 small eggs
1 tbsp oil
100 g brocciu

Put a little warm water and a pinch of sugar into a small bowl and add the yeast. Cover it with a cloth and leave to rise in a warm place for 15 minutes. Sift the flour and salt into a bowl and make a well in the centre. Beat the eggs and add them and the oil to the flour and mix together. Add enough water to make a fairly thick batter, stirring in the flour from the side of the bowl. Stir in the yeast mixture and leave to rise again in a warm place, covered with a cloth, for about 2 hours. Cut the *brocciu* into small cubes and stir carefully into batter. Drop teaspoonfuls of batter into hot oil or lard, making sure each spoonful contains a cube of cheese. As soon as they turn golden brown drain them on kitchen paper. Dredge with sugar and serve hot or cold.

POTATO FRITTERS

Fritelle di pommi

1 kilo potatoes
500 g plain flour
4 eggs, beaten
4 tbsp sugar
1 tbsp grated lemon or orange zest (unwaxed)
2 tbsp eau de vie *or other liqueur (optional)*
milk
sugar to dredge

Boil or steam the potatoes in lightly salted water. Peel them and mash with a ricer, or put them through a food mill. Add the flour, beaten eggs, sugar, zest and liqueur, if you are using any. Mix everything together well. If the mixture is very stiff add a little milk. It should have the consistency of a thick cake mix. Leave to stand for one hour. Drop spoonfuls into medium-hot deep oil and fry until golden, turning once. Drain on kitchen paper and dredge with sugar before serving.

SWISS CHARD AND RAISIN FRITTERS

Panzarotti di centuri

Here is a recipe for a different sort of fritter, made in Centuri, a fishing village in Cap Corse, the northern part of the island. It is a sort of fried ravioli stuffed with an unusual combination of Swiss chard and raisins and soaked in a syrup made from *arbouse*, the fruit of the strawberry tree, *Arbutus*. You could substitute redcurrant or quince jelly.

200 g plain flour
1 egg
50 g sugar
2 rounded tbsp lard
up to 2 tbsp eau de vie *or water*
pinch of salt
For the stuffing:
500 g Swiss chard (green parts only)
50 g raisins
grated zest of 1 lemon (unwaxed)
1 tbsp arbouse *jelly*
eau de vie, *rum or water to soak raisins*
For the syrup:
4 tbsp arbouse *jelly*
2 tbsp water

Sift the flour and salt into a bowl and rub the lard in with your fingertips. Add the sugar and beaten egg and mix with a fork. Add just enough liquid to hold the pastry together and form it into a ball. Cover and leave to rest. Soak the raisins in warm water or liquor for 1 hour. Cook the chard in a little lightly salted water for 10 minutes and strain. When cool enough to handle, squeeze to get rid of any liquid. Chop finely and mix with the drained raisins, lemon zest, jelly and 1 tablespoonful of the liquor from the raisins.

Roll the pastry out thinly on a lightly floured board. Cut into oblong shapes twice as long as wide and put a teaspoon of filling on one end of each oblong. Wet the edges with a little water and fold in half to make ravioli shapes. Press the edges together. Make sure the filling goes almost to the edges as the *panzarotti* will swell up when fried. For the syrup, heat the jelly and water together in a small pan and cool slightly. Fry the *panzarotti* in hot but not smoking oil until golden, turning them once. Drain on kitchen paper, then dip into the syrup, dredge with sugar, and serve warm with extra sugar.

APPLE GALETTES

Fritelle de mella

1 kilo apples (Granny Smith)
flour
4 eggs
100 g sugar
1 tsp baking powder
2 tbsp Calvados (optional)

Grate washed, unpeeled apples into a bowl. Add just enough flour to hold the fruit together. Beat eggs with sugar, baking powder and Calvados, then add to apple mixture. Heat a very little oil in a frying-pan and test fry a spoonful. If it doesn't hold together well, add a little more flour. It is better to add more flour than put in too much in the first place. Fry spoonfuls until golden brown on both sides. Drain on kitchen paper.

PUMPKIN AND RAISIN GALETTES

Fritelle di zucca e uvi seccati

Grate 1 kilogram of pumpkin flesh, then prepare and cook in the same way as the apple galettes. Add a handful of raisins that you have previously soaked in *eau de vie* or kirsch.

NEW YEAR'S DAY CAKE

Strennu du jour de l'an

Traditionally made to be served on New Year's Day.

For the pastry:
400 g plain flour
pinch salt
1 tbsp sugar
150 g butter
3 egg yolks
a little milk to bind
For the filling:
200 g brocciu
2 eggs
100 g sugar
grated zest of 1 orange
1 liqueur glass eau de vie

To make the pastry, sift the flour, salt and sugar into a bowl and rub the butter in with your fingertips. Add two of the egg yolks and just enough milk to bind the pastry together. Form into two equal balls, cover and leave to rest for 30 minutes. Meanwhile make the filling.

Crush the *brocciu* with a fork and mix well with other ingredients. Roll out the two pieces of pastry very thinly and cut into circles with the aid of a large plate. Put the filling in the centre of one leaving a border of plain pastry. Brush the edges with a little milk and cover with the second piece of pastry. Pinch the edges together firmly and brush the surface of the pie with the third egg yolk mixed with a little water. Cook in a preheated oven (200°C/gas 6) for 25 to 30 minutes.

DEAD MEN'S BREAD

Pan di i morti

The recipe comes from Bonifacio; it used to be made for All Saints' Day, when the doors and windows of all the houses were left open, the fires lit and food and drink left out so that the spirits of the dead could eat, drink and warm themselves before returning to 'the other side'. More importantly, they would not disturb the living with complaints about being hungry and thirsty in the dead of night.

Although this tradition has now fallen into disuse, the bread is still made and sold in bakers' shops all the year round in the south of the island. It makes a good accompaniment to cheese.

25 g fresh yeast
1 wine glass warm water
pinch of salt
800 g strong flour
2 eggs
250 g sugar
175 g soft butter
grated zest of 1 lemon (unwaxed)
250 g raisins
250 g hazelnuts

Mix the yeast with a pinch of salt and half the water and leave in a warm place until it starts to froth. Sift the flour into a bowl and add the butter, eggs, sugar, dissolved yeast and grated lemon zest. Knead well, adding as much more water as gives a soft, malleable dough. Cover with a cloth and leave to rise in a warm place for three hours. Work in the nuts and raisins and leave to rise, again covered with a cloth, for one hour or until approximately doubled in size. Shape into two or three round breads, put on an oiled baking tray, cover once more with a floured cloth, and let rise until two-thirds as large again. Brush the tops with the yolk of an egg mixed with a little water, and cook in a preheated oven (220°C/gas 7) for 40 minutes. Cool on a rack.

WHITE WINE BISCUITS

Canistrelli

You can find packets of these on the shelves of any supermarket or baker in Corsica. Traditionally flavoured with white wine or aniseed, now they are made with orange, lemon, almond, hazelnuts, chestnut flour and even chocolate chips. Here is the basic recipe.

5 g dried yeast
1 egg, beaten
600 g plain flour
150 g softened butter or (traditionally) lard
65 g sugar
½ glass white wine
25 g ground almonds

Mix the yeast with a little warm water and leave in a warm place for a few minutes to get frothy. Beat the egg. Sift the flour into a bowl and make a well in the centre. Add all the other ingredients and mix together lightly with your fingers. Form into a ball adding a little water if necessary. The dough should be quite firm. Leave to rise, covered, in a warm place from 1 ½ to 2 hours. Roll the dough out on a lightly floured board to the thickness of a finger. With a pastry cutter or sharp knife cut into smallish squares and oblongs. Place on an oiled baking tray and bake in a preheated oven (200°C/gas 6) for between 30 and 40 minutes until golden. Sometimes they are sprinkled with sugar before baking.

ANISEED BISCUITS

Canistri finuchietti

These little biscuits are nibbled at any time of the day, with coffee, tea or other drinks. Because there is no sugar in them they are often given to babies when they are teething.

25 g fresh yeast
500 g plain flour
pinch salt
1 tbsp whole aniseed
approximately ½ litre tepid water

Mix the yeast with a little warm water and leave for 10 minutes to get frothy. Sift the flour and salt into a bowl and add the yeast and aniseed grains. Add enough water to make a firm dough and knead well for several minutes. Cut into 20 equal pieces, roll out each piece to a sausage shape the diameter of a little finger, sufficiently long to then form into a figure of eight, wetting both ends to seal them together. Heat a large saucepan of boiling water and drop the *canistri* into it. Do not crowd the pan. Simmer until they float to the surface and take out with a slotted spoon or spatula. Drain on a clean cloth or kitchen paper. Meanwhile, heat the oven to 230°C/gas 8. Put the *canistri* on a greased baking tray and bake for 10 minutes.

GRAPE JUICE BISCUITS

U biscuitellu

1 litre grape juice
200 g sugar
5 g dried yeast
600 g plain flour
pinch of salt
1 tbsp pastis
$^{1}/_{2}$ tsp ground nutmeg

Boil the grape juice in a saucepan until it has reduced to a quarter of its volume, stir in the sugar and leave to get cold. Mix the yeast with a little warm water and leave for 10 minutes to get frothy. Sift the flour and salt into a bowl and add all the other ingredients. Knead everything together very well and leave, covered, in a warm place for two hours or until it has doubled in volume. Form into small cylindrical shapes about 6 cms long and put on an oiled baking tray. Cook in a preheated oven (220°C/gas 7) for 30 minutes. These biscuits are traditionally cooked on chestnut leaves that have been soaked in water for a couple of hours.

ALMOND MACAROONS
Marzipani

300 g almonds with their inner skins
600 g sugar
6 egg whites
pinch salt
1 scraped vanilla pod, or vanilla essence

Pound the almonds with their skins in a mortar or food processor. Mix with the sugar, which will soak up the oil from the almonds. Add the vanilla. Beat the egg whites with a pinch of salt until they are fairly stiff and stir about 2 tbsp into the almond mixture to loosen it. Gradually stir in the rest. Put spoonfuls of the mixture on sugared greaseproof paper or rice paper, and cook in a preheated cool oven (150°C/gas 2) for 30 to 35 minutes, until the macaroons are pale gold in colour.

FLOATING ISLANDS

Iles flottantes Serves 6

This recipe is for a dessert familiar to everyone on the French mainland; and so too is the one that follows. However, I have included them here because they turn up time and again on Corsican menus.

8 eggs
1 vanilla pod
1 litre full-cream milk
300 g, plus 2 tbsp sugar
12 lumps sugar

Separate the eggs. Split the vanilla pod and scrape the seeds into the milk. Put the milk, with the split vanilla pod, into a pan and bring to the boil. Take off the heat. Beat the egg yolks with 200 grams of sugar in a bowl over boiling water until the mixture is pale and thick. Remove the vanilla pod and pour the hot milk, stirring constantly, into the egg mixture. Continue to cook on the double-boiler until it thickens. Do not let it boil. Pour into a serving dish and let it cool.

The custard done, whisk the egg whites with a pinch of salt until they are stiff. Whisk in 50 grams of the sugar and then fold in another 50 grams. Bring a wide pan of water (seasoned with 2 tbsp sugar) to a simmering boil. Poach large spoonfuls of the egg whites in the water for 2 minutes, turning them over once. Drain and place at regular intervals over the top of the custard. Melt the sugar lumps in a small saucepan with 2 tbsp water until caramelized. Carefully dribble over the egg whites. Serve chilled. You can replace the caramel with melted chocolate if you prefer.

SAVOIE BISCUIT
U pan di Spagna

The name in Corsican means 'Spanish bread'. It is served at all festive occasions, decorated with icing sugar or chocolate

150 g sugar
4 eggs, separated
60 g plain flour
60 g potato flour

Beat the sugar and egg yolks together until they are almost white. Fold in the two flours very carefully with a whisk. Beat egg whites with a pinch of salt until stiff and carefully fold into mixture. Put into a buttered, fluted mould (such as are used for *kugelhopf*) or sponge-cake tin and bake in preheated oven (200°C/gas 6) for 35 or 40 minutes, until a knife inserted in the centre comes out clean. Turn out straightaway and, when cool, cover with melted chocolate, icing sugar or glacé icing. Decorate with coloured icing if you wish.

PRESERVES

FIG JAM
Confiturra di fiche

1 kilo figs
$^1/_2$ kilo sugar, $^1/_2$ litre water

Wash the figs without breaking them. Bring the water and sugar to the boil. When bubbles start to appear on the surface, put in the figs. Cook gently for 1 $^1/_2$ hours. The figs will become transparent. Ladle the figs and syrup into sterilized jars and cover with circles of greaseproof paper. Leave to cool before putting on the lids and labelling.

FRUIT IN GRAPE JELLY

Confiturra d'uva

2 kilos black grapes
sugar
2 pears
2 apples
100 g walnut pieces or hazelnuts

Wash the grapes and put them through a food mill, or press through a sieve fine enough to keep out the pips and skins. Weigh the resulting juice and measure out two-thirds of the weight in sugar. Before you add the sugar, however, bring the juice to a boil and reduce by half. Meanwhile peel and core the fruit and cut into eighths. Add the sugar, nuts and fruit to the juice and simmer for about 45 minutes or until the jam is ready to set. Skim the froth from the top from time to time as the jam is cooking. Test if the jam is setting by letting a spoonful cool on a saucer. If a skin can be seen when you pull your little finger across the surface, the jam is ready. Let it cool slightly and put into sterilized jars. Cover the tops with circles of greaseproof paper and let cool before putting the lids on and labelling.

ARBOUSE JELLY
Confiturra di bagu

The strawberry tree or *Arbutus* forms part of the *maquis* which covers so much of the island. It is a very pretty tree with both fruit and flowers hanging from its branches at the same time. The flowers are white and the fruit ranges in colour from pale green through golden orange to scarlet. The fruit is used to make both a liqueur and a jelly.

2 kilos arbouses
sugar

Wash the fruit and put in a saucepan and almost cover with cold water. Bring to the boil and then simmer for 10 minutes. Strain through a muslin cloth, pressing with a wooden spoon to extract all the juice. Weigh the juice and add the same weight of sugar. Simmer the juice and sugar together until ready to set, skimming the froth off the top regularly. Test for setting as above. Ladle the jelly into sterilized jars and cover the tops with rounds of greaseproof paper. Put on the lids and label when cold.

CEDRAT CONFIT
Alimea cunfettu

Cedrats, which are a variety of citron, have been cultivated in Corsica for hundreds of years. At the end of the nineteenth century the island produced thousands of tons every year. A large part of the production was exported, either in a *saumure* (a brine pickle) or crystallized in sugar. Corsican cedrats contain little or no acid, which is unique among cultivated cedrats. Here is the method for crystallizing them. I am giving the recipe for one kilo of fruit but it is so time-consuming it would be better to treat several kilos at the same time. If you can't find cedrats use thick-skinned lemons or uglis.

1 kilo cedrats
1 1/2 kilos sugar

Cut the cedrats in half vertically, remove the pips, and soak in cold water for three days, changing the water morning and evenings. Change the water again and cook the cedrats until they are just soft. Take them out of the water and plunge them into cold water for one minute. Drain them and leave to dry on a clean cloth until the next day. Mix the sugar with one litre of water in a large saucepan and bring to the boil. When it boils, put in the fruit and simmer for 15 minutes. Take the fruit out and put it in a china or Pyrex dish. The next day, bring the syrup back to the boil and add the fruit. Boil for five minutes, remove the fruit and put back into bowl. Repeat this operation for the next 8 days. The last day remove the fruit and bring the syrup back to the boil. Pour over the cedrats, let them drain and leave to dry in the sun or in a very low oven.

PEACH RATAFIA

Ratavia de preshe

Ratafias, fruits conserved in alcohol, are often served at the end of a meal, particularly when there are guests or on special occasions. They are usually made with an *eau de vie* but if you don't have any, you can use 90° alcohol diluted with the same amount of cold, boiled water. That instruction is not so easy to follow in Britain where, of course, you can use vodka straight from the bottle. Ratafias can be made with fresh or dried fruit, although the dried has more flavour.

1 kilo small firm ripe peaches
1 litre eau de vie *or vodka*
250 g sugar
1/2 litre water

Wash the peaches and prick them all over with a needle, through to the kernel. Soak them in cold water for 15 minutes and then dry them. Heat the water and sugar together in a large saucepan until the sugar dissolves. Simmer for 2 minutes and put in the peaches. Bring back to the boil and let the syrup bubble twice. Turn the fruit if necessary to make sure it is covered and then remove it with a slotted spoon to a covered dish. Leave overnight. The next day, reheat and reduce the syrup a little. Put the fruit back and bring to the boil. Remove the peaches again and replace in the covered dish overnight. The third day, put the peaches into a sterilized jar. Mix the syrup and alcohol together and pour over the fruit. Put a lid on the jar and keep for three months before eating and drinking.

PRUNE RATAFIA

Ratavia di prugnelle secche

750 g dried prunes
150 g sugar
1 litre eau de vie

Either soak the prunes for several hours in an infusion of weak tea or plunge them into boiling water for 1 minute. Dry them well and put them into a sterilized jar. Mix the sugar with the *eau de vie* and pour it over. Seal hermetically and give the jar a shake to make sure it is well mixed. This *ratafia* can be used after a month but the longer you leave it the better it tastes!

A NOTE ABOUT BOOKS

Association A. Mimoria, sous la direction de Lucette Poncin, *Noëls de Corse, Natali Corsi*, Edisud, 1998.

C.N.A.C., *L'Inventaire du patrimoine culinaire de la France (Région Corse)*, Albin Michel, 1996.

'Cuisine du bout du monde: saveurs corses', *Voyager*, No 19.

Alan Davidson, *Mediterranean Seafood*, Penguin, 1972; reprinted, Prospect Books, 2002.

Maria Nunza Filipinni, *La Cuisine corse*, La Marge-Alto, 1978.

Brigitte et Jean-Pierre Perrin-Chattard, *Mieux connaître la cuisine corse*, Jean-Paul Gisserot, 1999.

F. Ricciardi-Bartoli, *Cuisine de Corse de A – Z*, Bonneton, 1997.

Christiane Schapira, *La Cuisine corse*, Solar, 1979.

Paul Silvani, *Cuisine corse d'antan*, La Marge, 1991.

INDEX